High Shelf

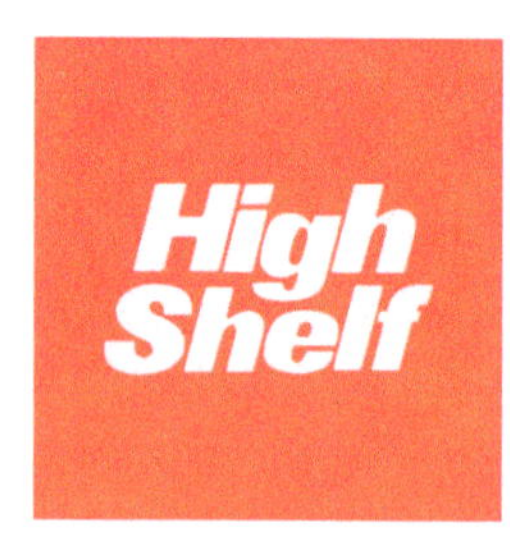

High Shelf XXVII. February 2021.

Portland, Oregon.

ISBN: 978-1-952869-25-9

Cover Image by Samuel Keith Bliss
Design and Layout by C. M. Tollefson
Editing by David Seung & C. M. Tollefson

With special thanks to:
Kelsey Beck Kuther, Megan Kim, & River Elizabeth Hall.

High Shelf XXVI

February 2021

"... let me teach you how to please me/let me show
you how to open my legs/just/like this/can you
see it/this is the part of me that is connected
straight to my brain/touch me here
and I'll/grow wings/touch me here
before the river of my body runs dry..."

Ann Pedone

"... He speeds forward. Direct as a thrust,
This young god is his own herald.
No need for exegesis.
He'll give it as it is

And take what he desires..."

Steven Van Pelt

Table Of Contents

Electricity

Katie O'Malley

From the Greek word "elektron," meaning "amber"

1. What I'd give to be encased in sap,
surrounded by sweet orange
with a constant view of the sunset.

2. We have always defined the sky
by the presence of light.
In stories we tell from
region to region to region
the world starts dark.

3. Mosquitoes are technically lightning bugs.
When they get close enough, you can hear them
buzz with static.

4. The Cicada whirs with industry,
clicks like wiring—
a regular machine—
and she gets to leave a shell behind
that looks at home stuck to a leaf
or half-buried in soil
or garnishing the bark of a maple tree.

5. Moths hang on light like bulbs on a circuit—
Glow to moth, moth to glow—
energy recycled between them.

6. I can't live and die like a bug.
My sparks start
fires and sugar softens
in my hands.

April Killed a Man

Seneca Basoalto

April killed a man, again / there were fourteen photographs
left on his phone that he had yet to publish

semolina and squalor, numbers written in chalk on the bathroom
wall of an arcade, an adequate score in vintage frames,
curdled Irish cream / no one else sees it, but
I think he wished he were electricity

he saw a murder of crows at sunrise on the farm
that once belonged to his grandfather, and he
struggled to recall the lyrics to the song once
hummed by the girl he once loved while
twining straws and wishing his love knew of
a different hue, entirely

half-rabid, pocket watch hieroglyphics,
an impending solstice
of poppies and homegrown candle wax

he never had the chance to fly into her window,

it's a long story / and we only know
what can be read in the news

June Corkscrew

Dualtagh McDonnell

Her accent seems stronger on these cheap olive green walls,
my mother and brothers travelling in search of a home filled in motion,
the yellow canopy covering the ceiling full of little shields
inflating and exhaling these words across the stone of the house.
The sky's utensils are hanging in the shelf of the weather as I listen to her voice.
and I think of this independence I find while left
to articulate study, repetition, globalisation
and I write on the half sides of paper
transcribing the solar system into an A4 divided.

Cushions and rugs on the worn down tiles,
mango juice and mints before the open mouth of an exam.
But these don't match: the heat, this cave called home
and this foreign school, first Peroni, newspaper formats and *i temi,*
and four green apples to have under the company of the tower.

Time before and after this is a rough
amalgam of wet and spotty life
but in the betweens, these dates gild the calendars
like little yellow parasols across the stone coloured sky.
Terracotta portions frame the boundaries
and hug the sky like we used to hug each other
with our talk and arguments and *let's run aways.*

And everything always lives there.
The trauma of a three day sea,
beginning to wane to understand the
glare of the moon.
This makes sense to us,
abstract and warm.

Edge Of The Earth

Kimberly Patino

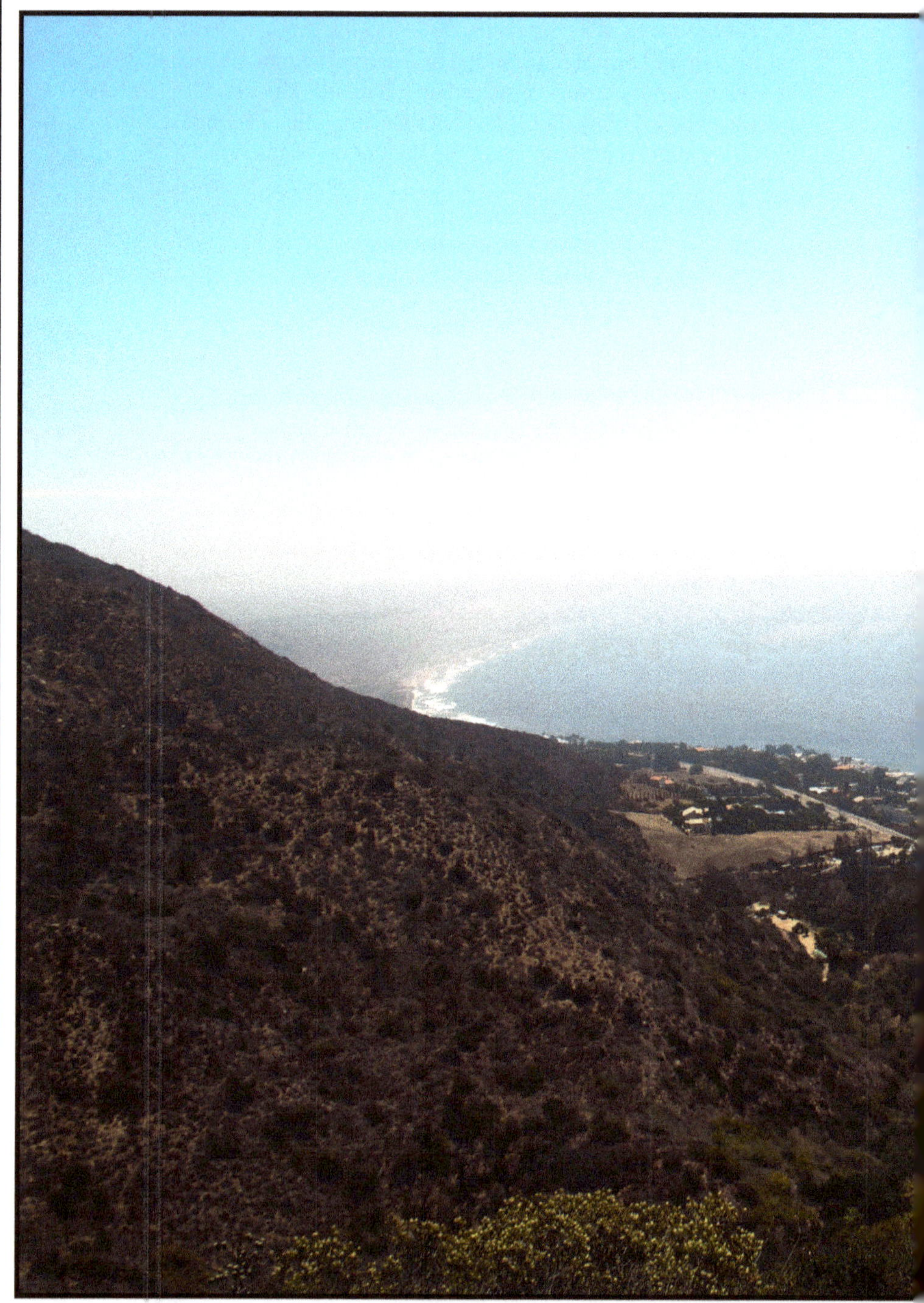

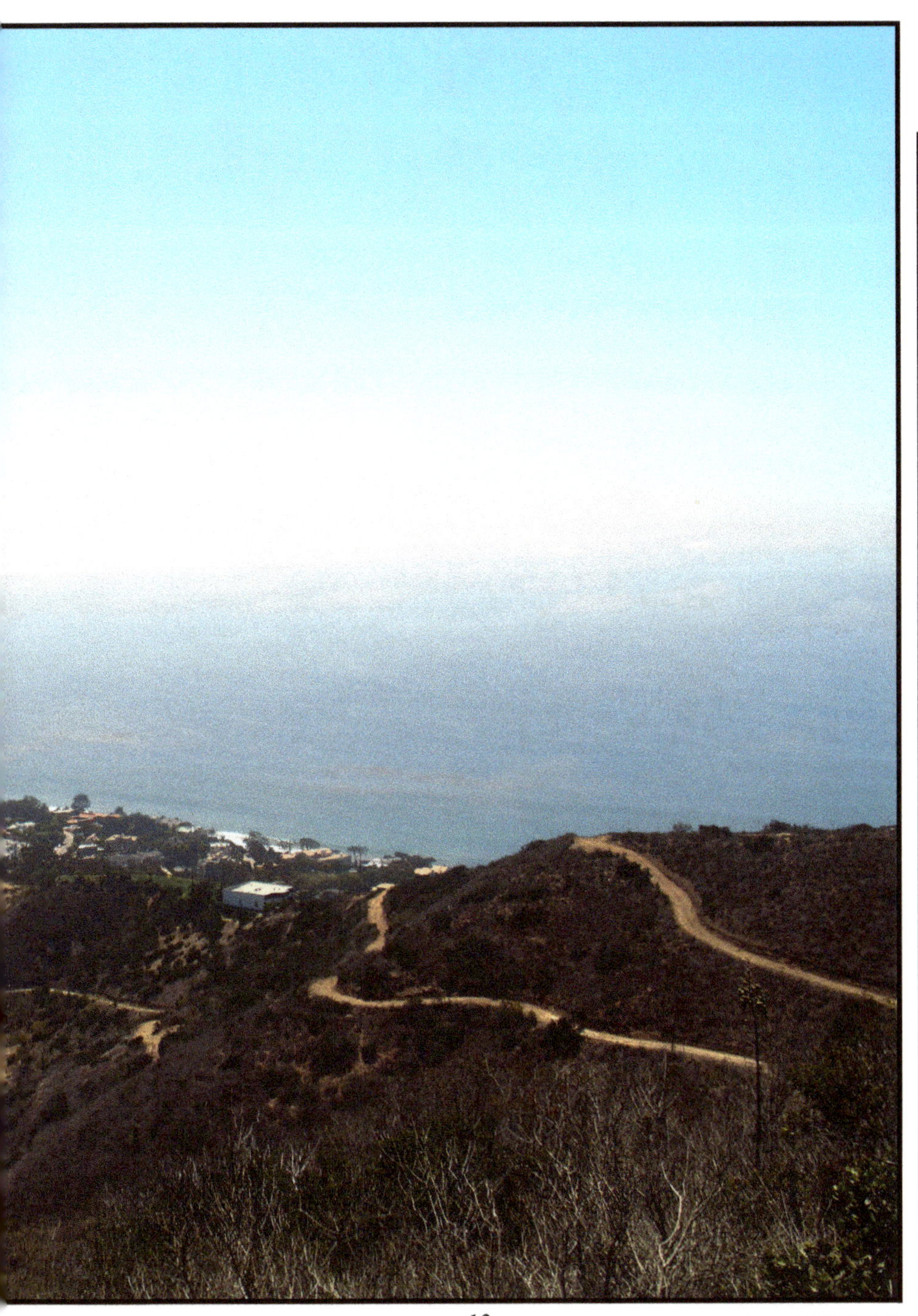

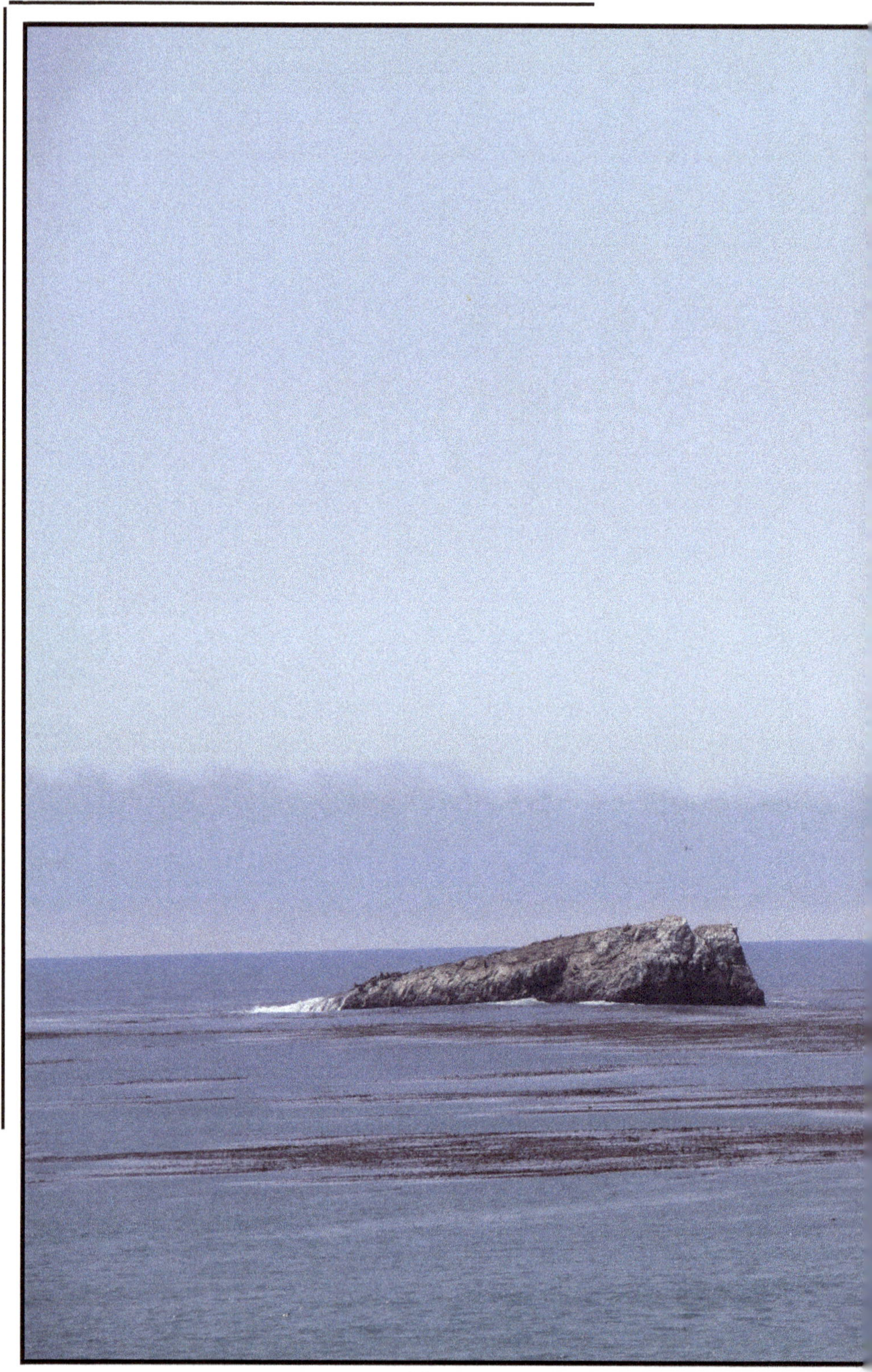

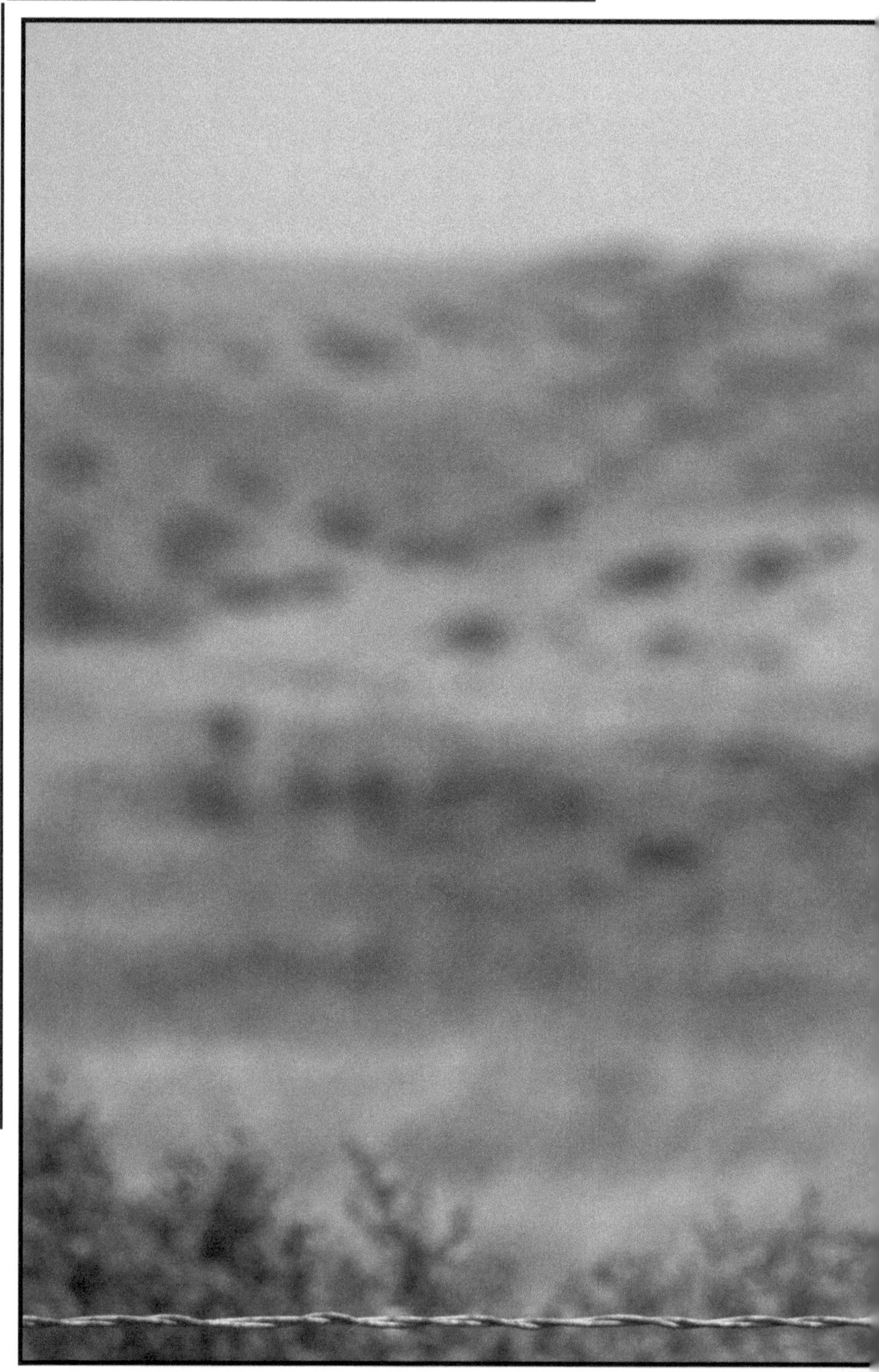

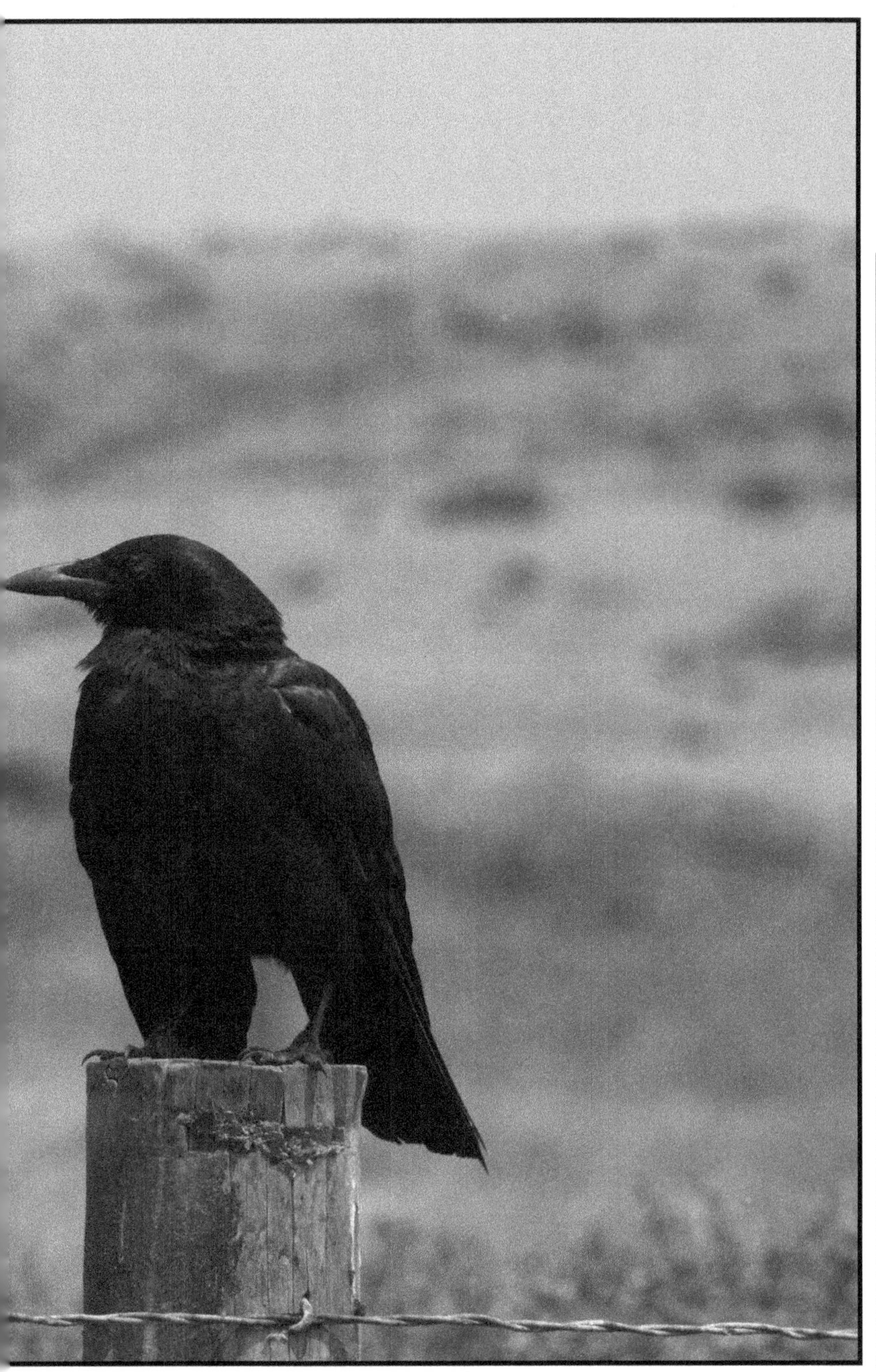

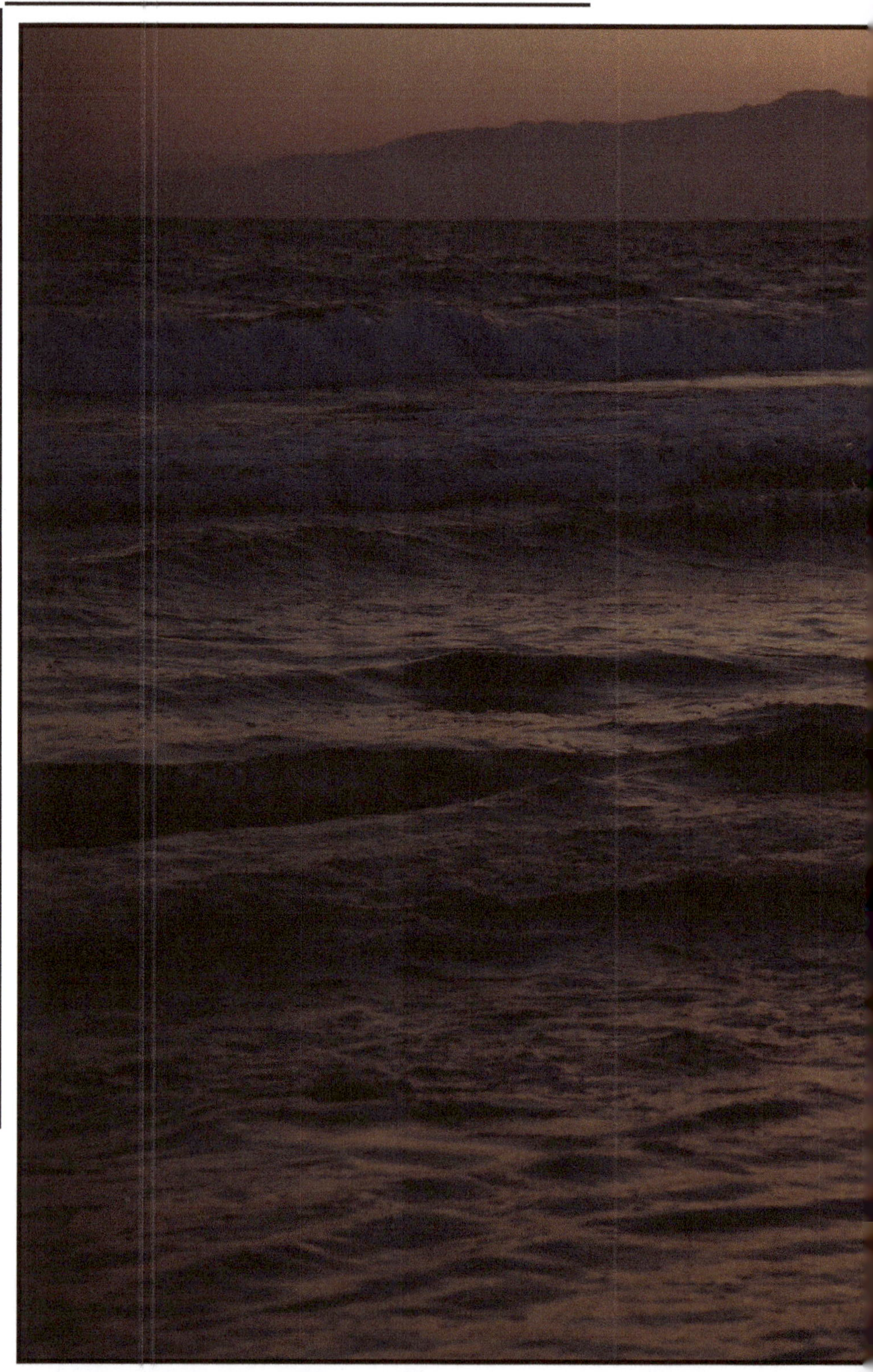

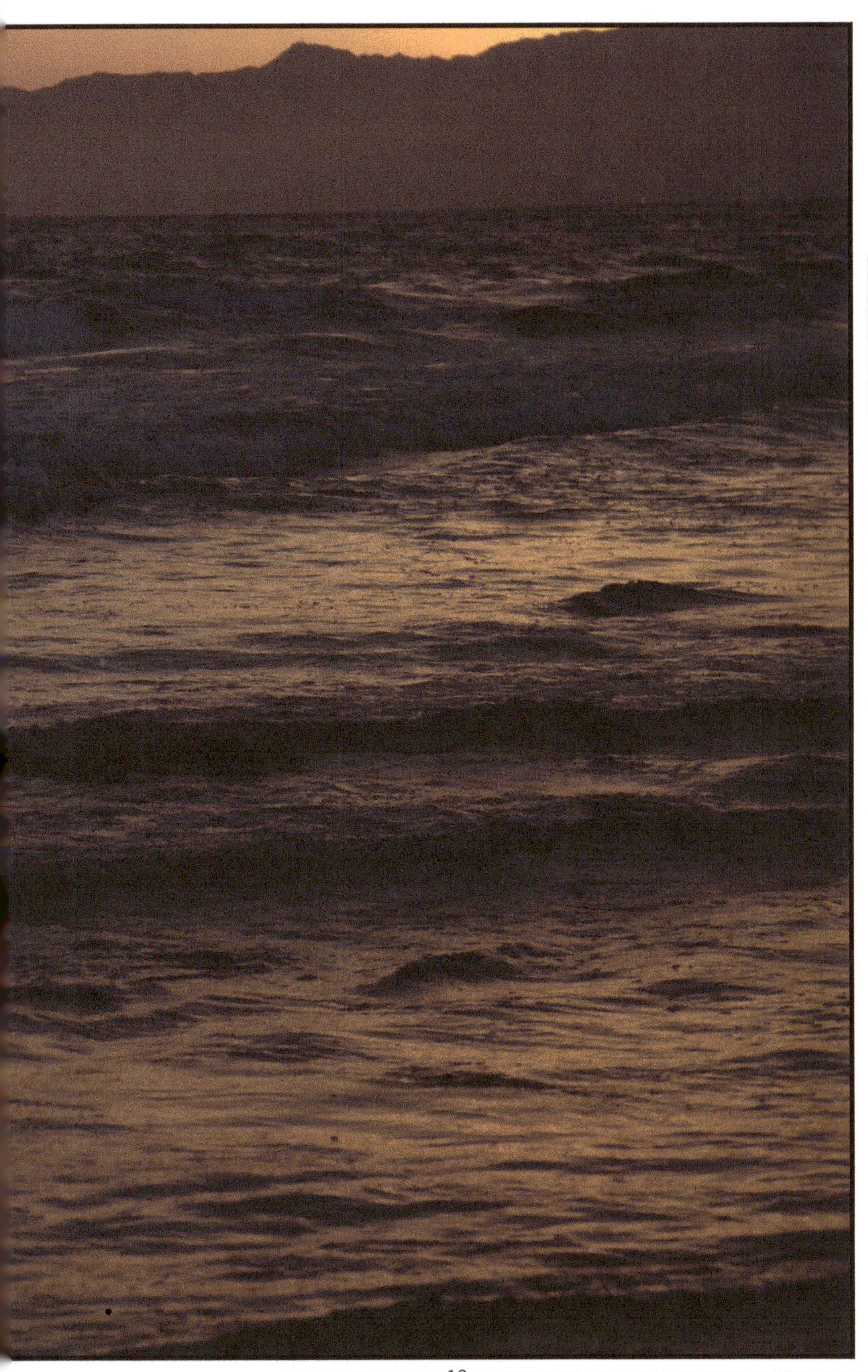

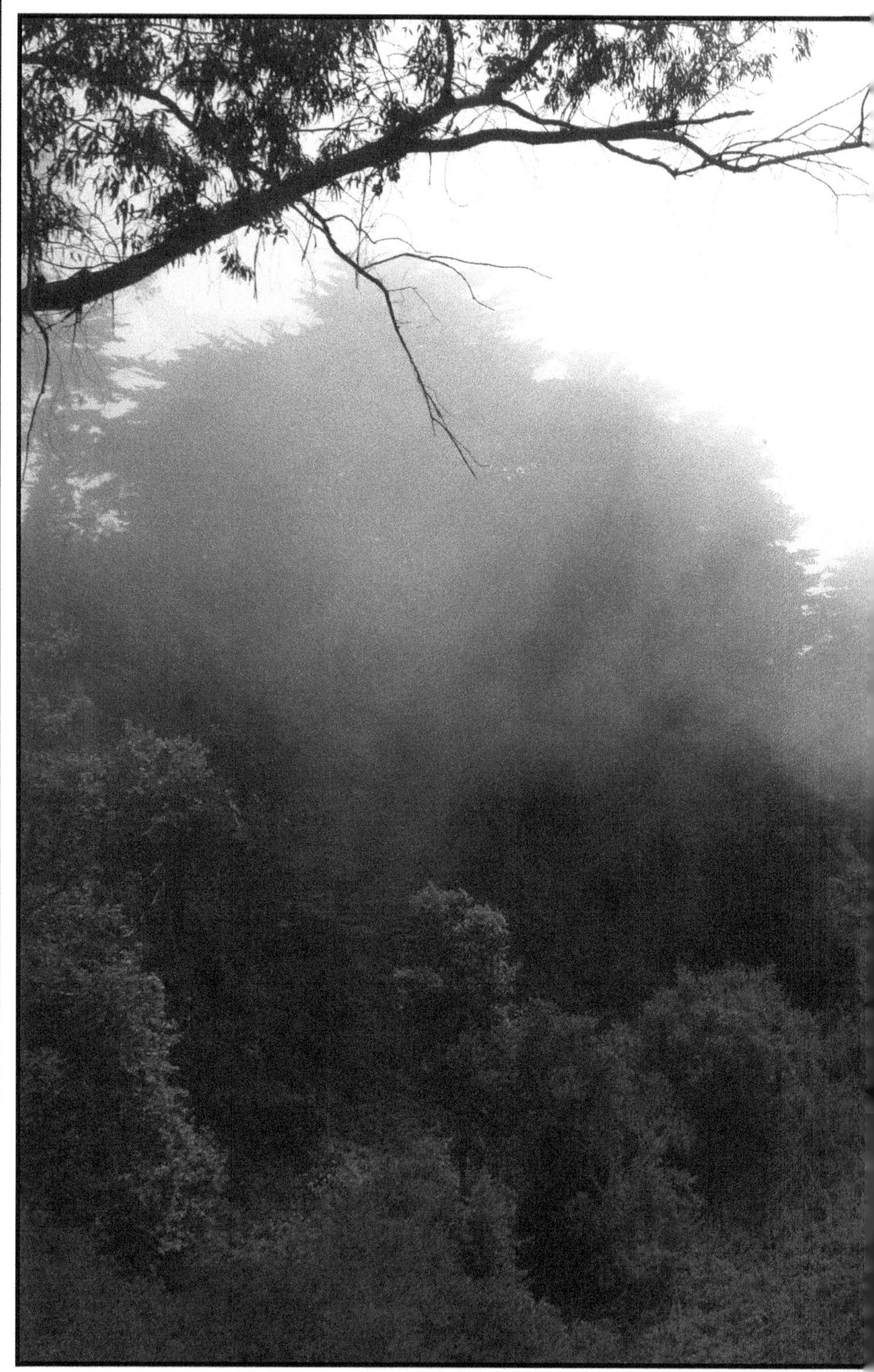

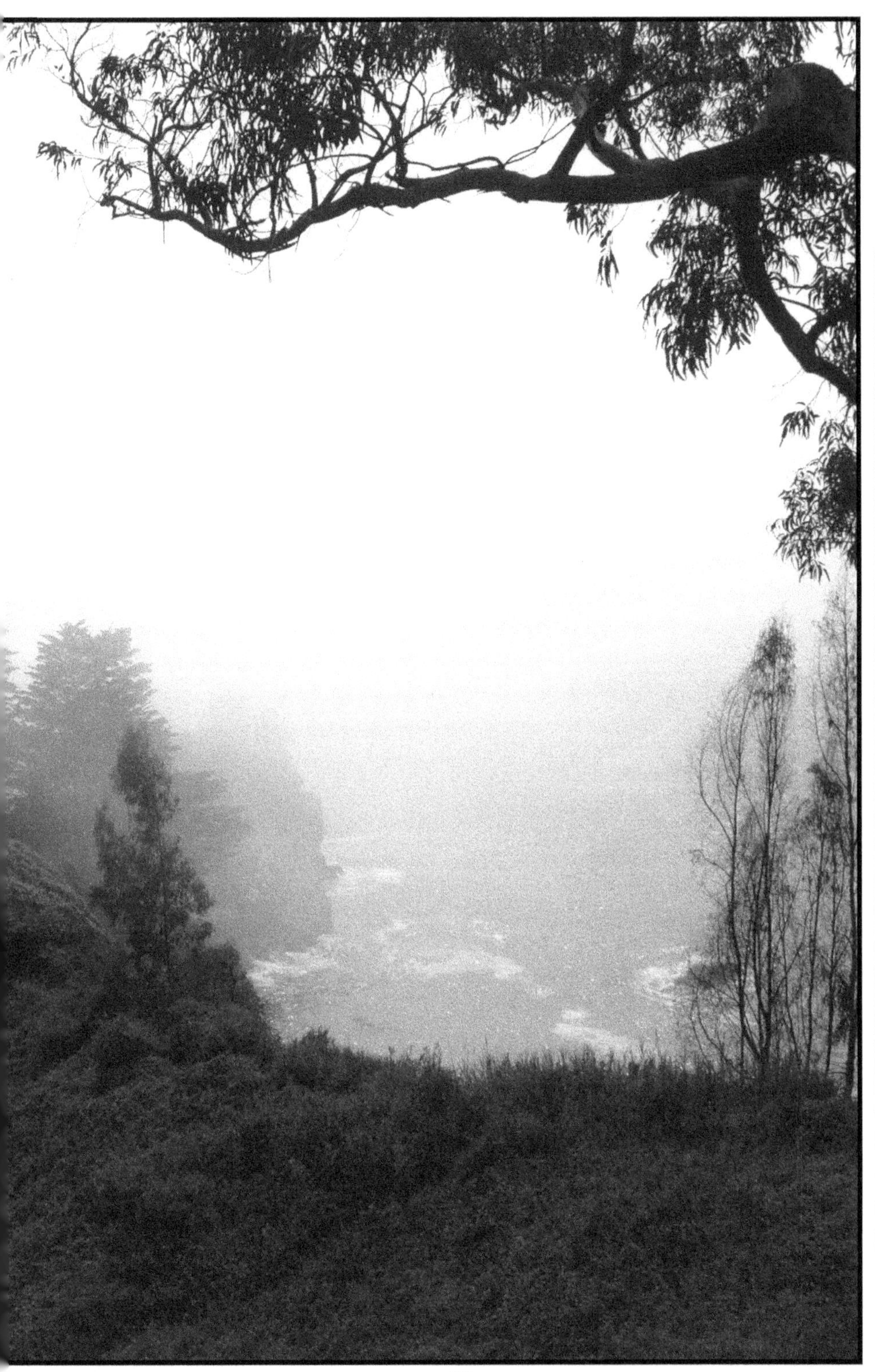

Picking Blueberries: a Guide

Signe E. Land

Picking blueberries is an art form. Outside in the sun,
sun in your eyes, sun burning your nose.
You must go

slowly. Cup your hand around a ripened bunch like
you would cup a lover's balls,
softly, delicate, velvet.

Finger the indigo ripe bursting berries like you would
a lover's swelling, glistening lips.
Palm them as they

fall gently from their stems into your waiting bowl. If
you practice, the unripe berries will stay
safely attached,

living to ripen another day. Eat as many as you save.
Tangy and wet. Your fingers and your
mouth will be stained

blue. All stories deserve to be told. Your teeth? Forget it.
Your dogs don't care about the color of your
teeth, or the tiny

black seeds stuck between them. Know that when
chickadees, finches and cardinals
eat blueberries they

will spread the tiny seeds, unasked, propagating more
bushes, more berries, while you just take,
and take, and take

tonguing juice, juice trickling from the corners of your
mouth, blue rivers down your chin. Ask:
Could you learn

to live like this? Offering, asking nothing in return? Imagine
you were a child with a kindly mother.
She calls out:

"Save some for the pies!" easy laughter in her voice, as
wasps buzz lazily, languid in and out of the
branches and purple

fecund glory, emerald leaves dancing *en masse* in the
hot, humid breeze, and your dog mouthing
low-hanging branches,

munching stem and berries alike. The bushes do not
worry about death. They spread *per stirpes*, by
their strong roots,

sister bushes entwined deep under the soil. Do not worry;
the unpicked berries you grieve today
will dry into hard

pea-sized seed balls, ready. Trust. Sweat rivulets down the
middle of your back. Seeds begetting
seeds begetting

seeds. Dream of soft tendrils, running water, fingers swirling
on damp skin, a woman's touch. Listen to the
story you hold

in your heart; nurse it tenderly as you wash your warm
bowl full of blueberries, your hands and
lips stained blue,

your fingers carefully brushing away bits of brown
stem and leaves. Can you learn to
live like this?

#17 (From Twenty-five Love Songs)

Ann Pedone

I believe in ghosts, I believe in luck and fate and destiny
I roll the dice whenever I get the chance
sometimes I count out beads on a rosary
I keep hidden/in a drawer
I've been to Paris/but I've never been
to Berlin/I fucked a man on the roof of a building
after a party once/I don't remember his
name/ sometimes I play dumb
I sometimes/don't know how to draw boundaries
sometimes I don't/cross my legs
I've been told I should see a therapist/remind me
again how you like your coffee
tell me when you are about to cum/don't make me
wait for it/tell me again that you want me more
than her/I won't say my body is like a rosary/but
sometimes/ it feels like one
let me teach you how to please me/let me show
you how to open my legs/just/like this/can you
see it/this is the part of me that is connected
straight to my brain/touch me here
and I'll/grow wings/touch me here
before the river of my body runs dry
I need to take a shower/I need to get on a
plane in an hour/I need to try harder
to forget his face
long before I was a woman I was a thing
burning in the middle of the sea
I was in the middle of the sea I closed
my eyes and mouthed the word *waves*
the water changed the shape of my body as only water can

Otherworldly and Vaguely Threatening

Kristen Herrington & Lyndsay Doyle

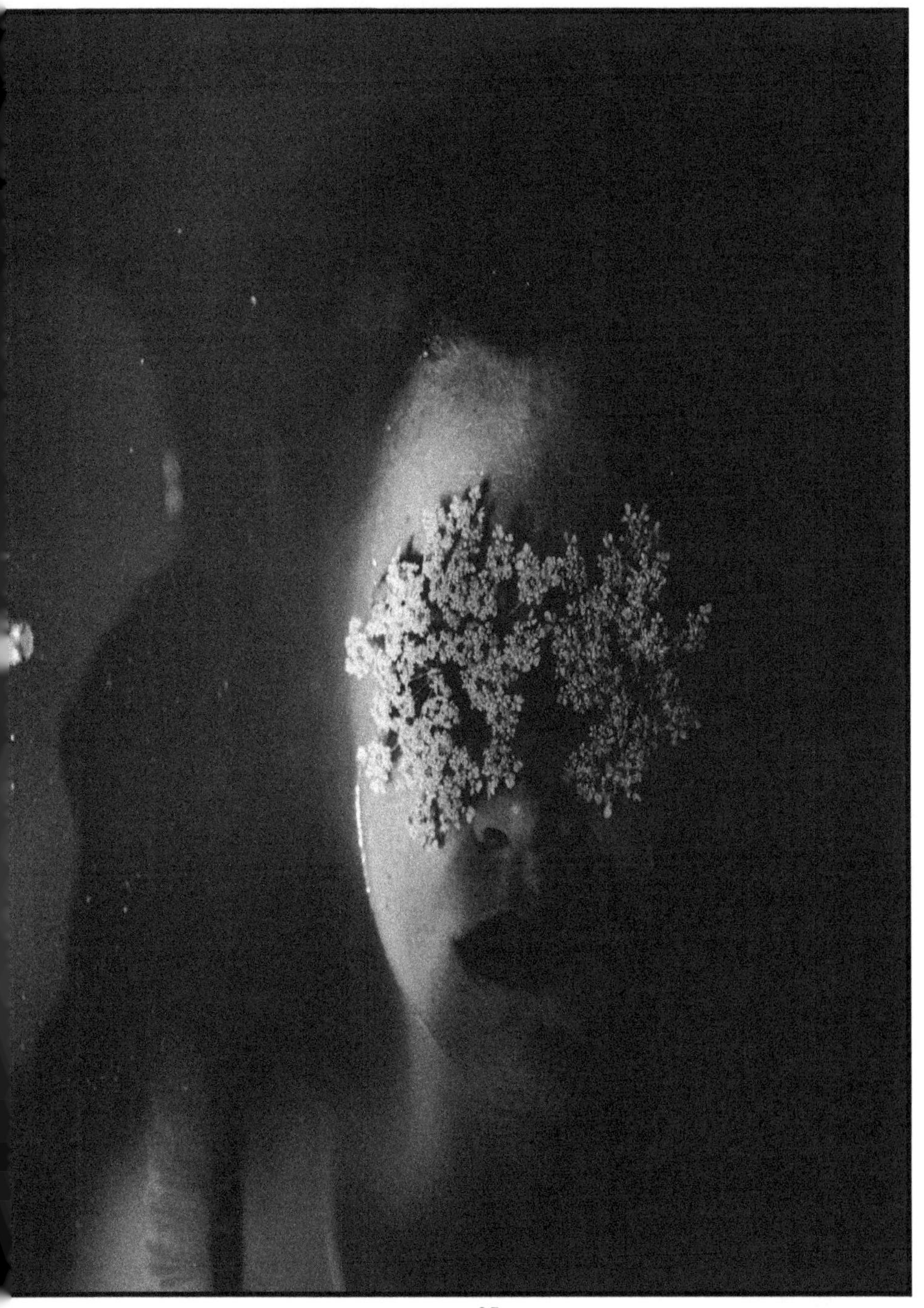

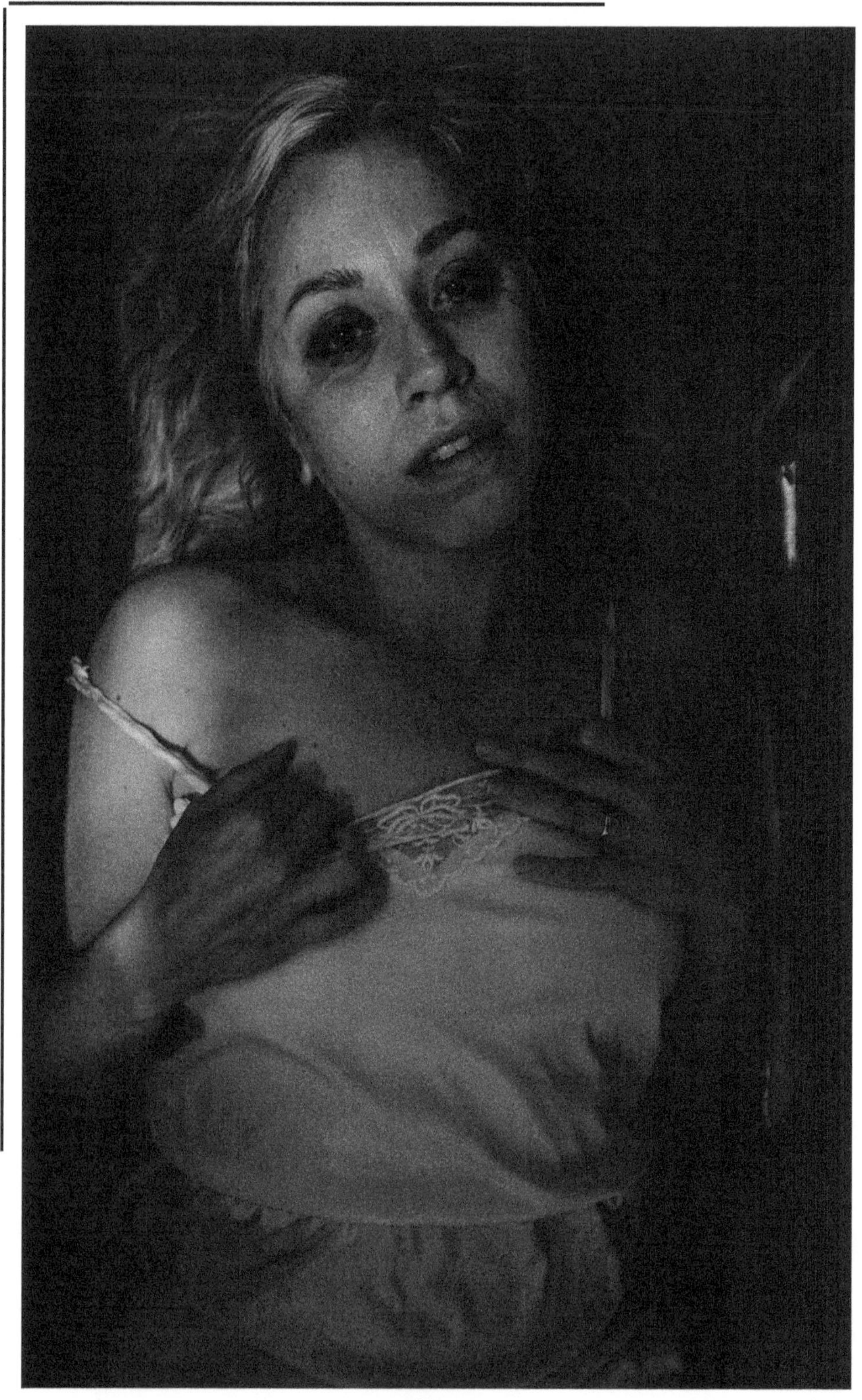

Haven

Samuel Keith Bliss

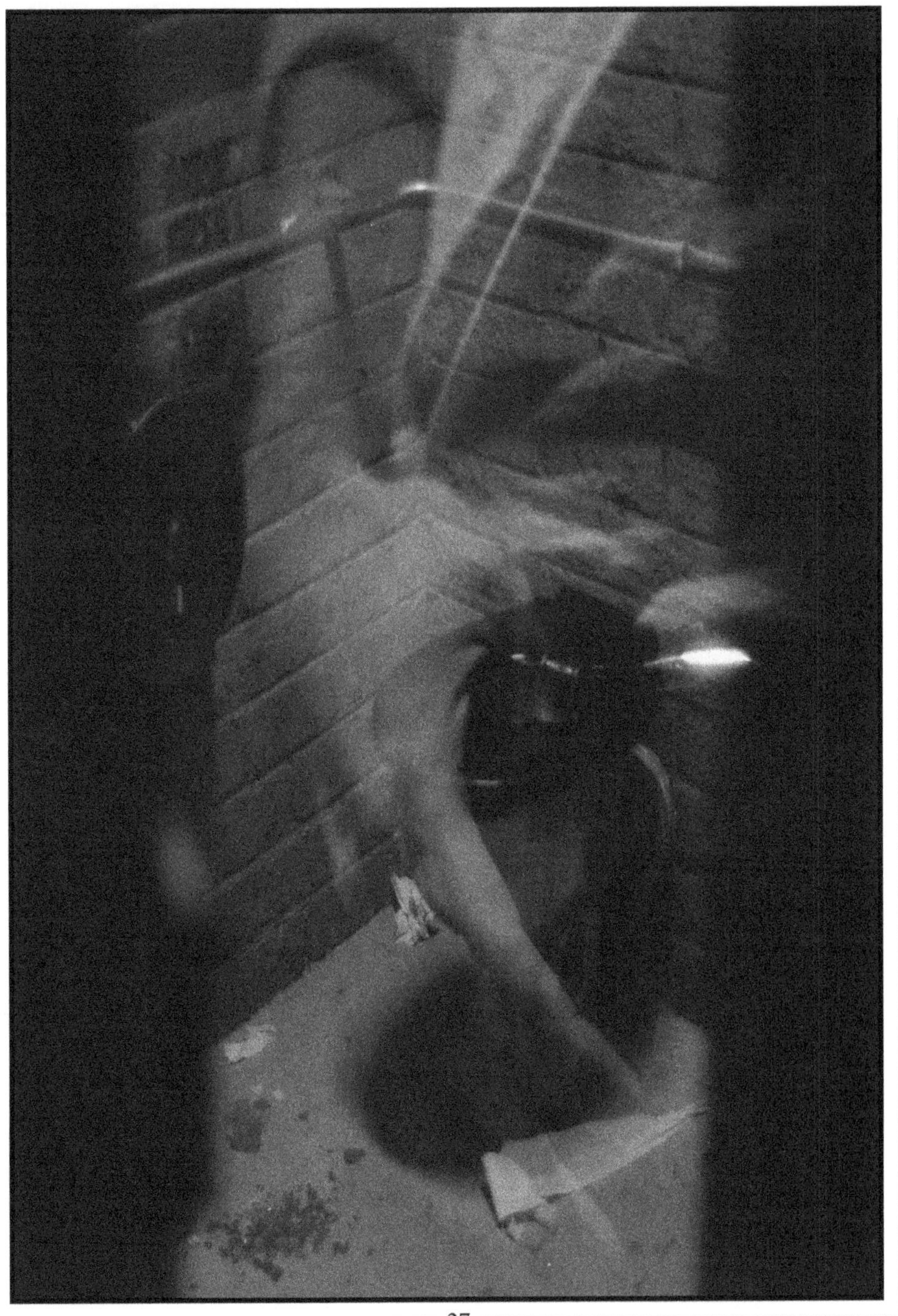

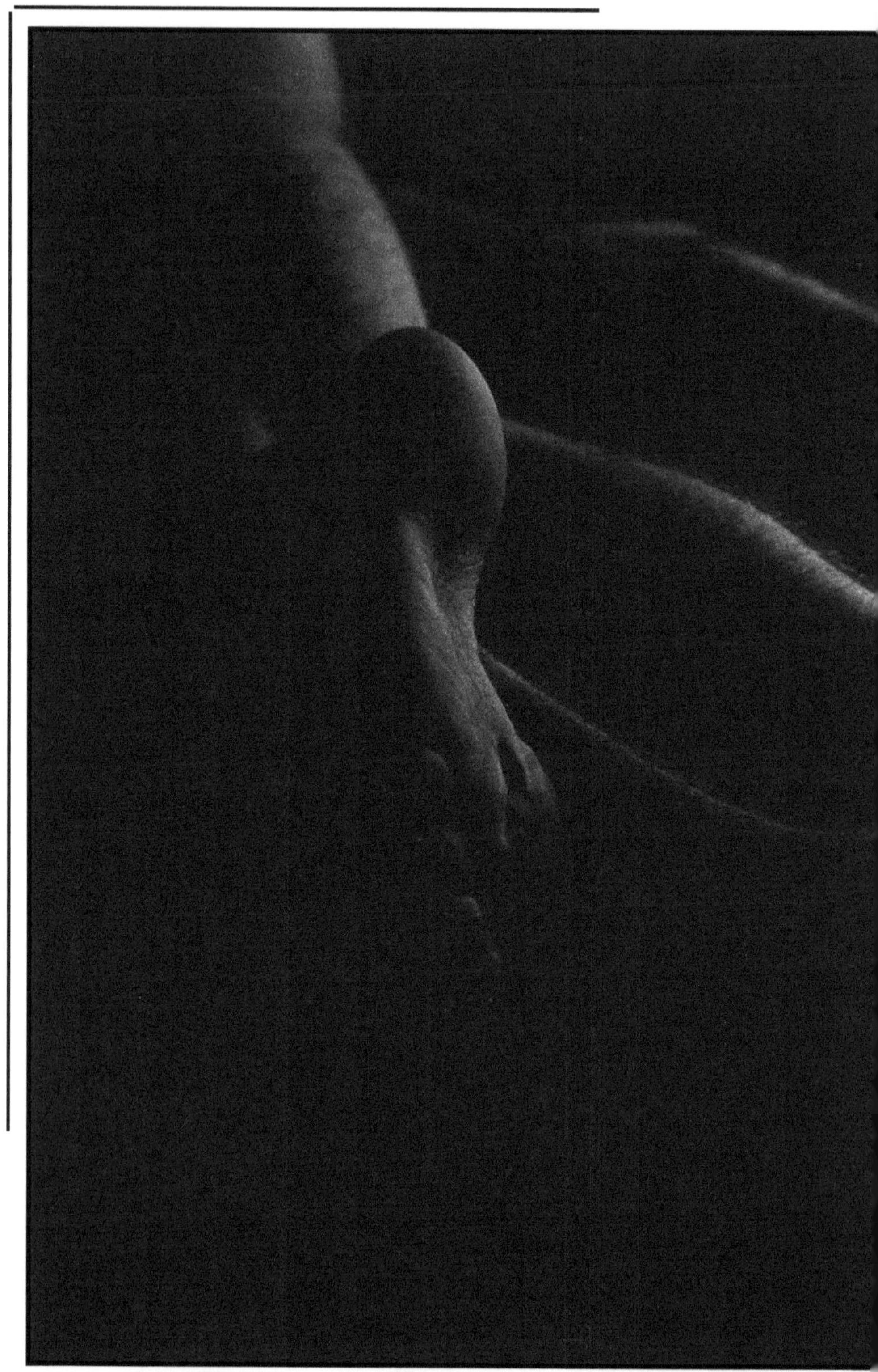

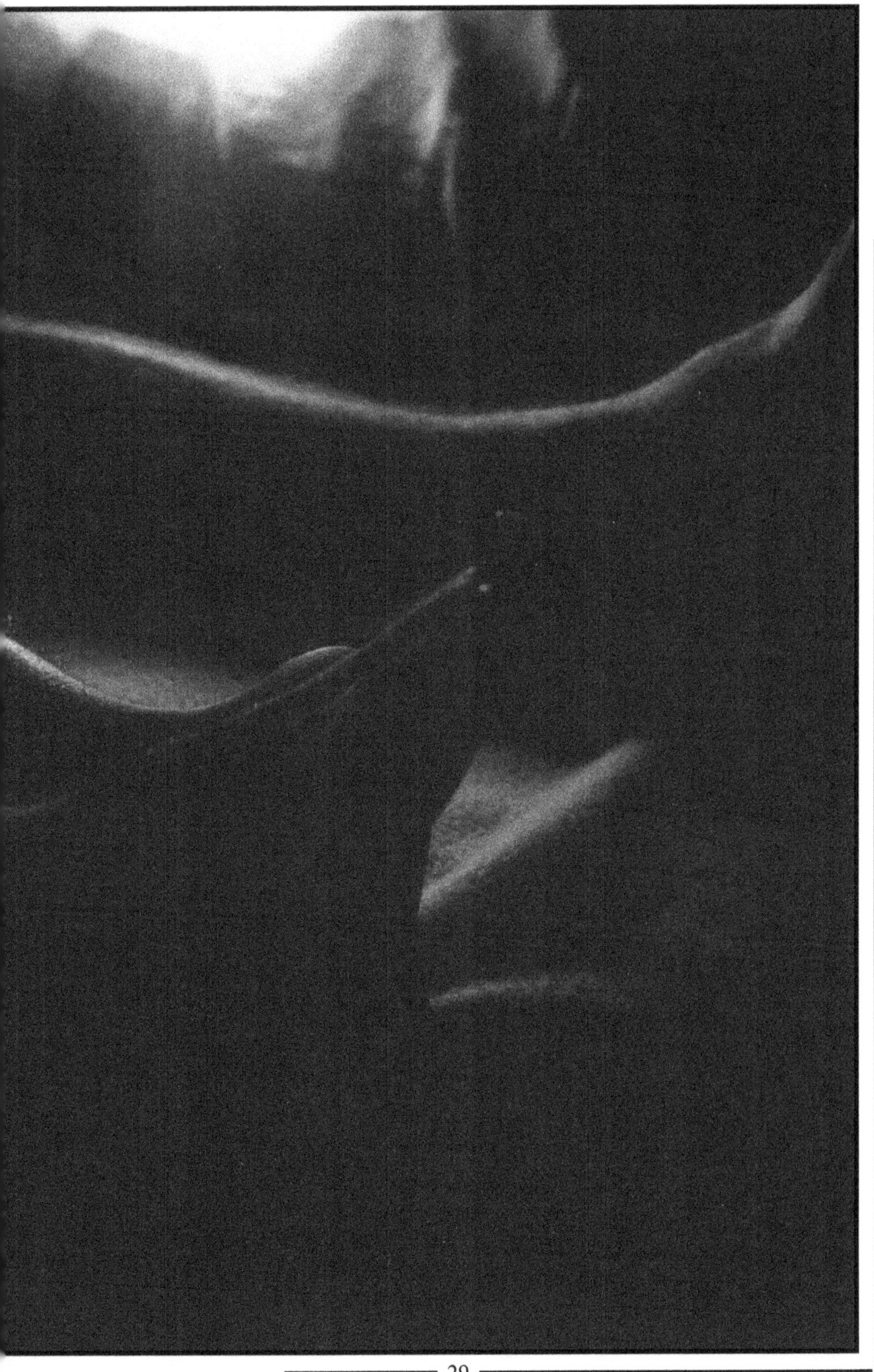

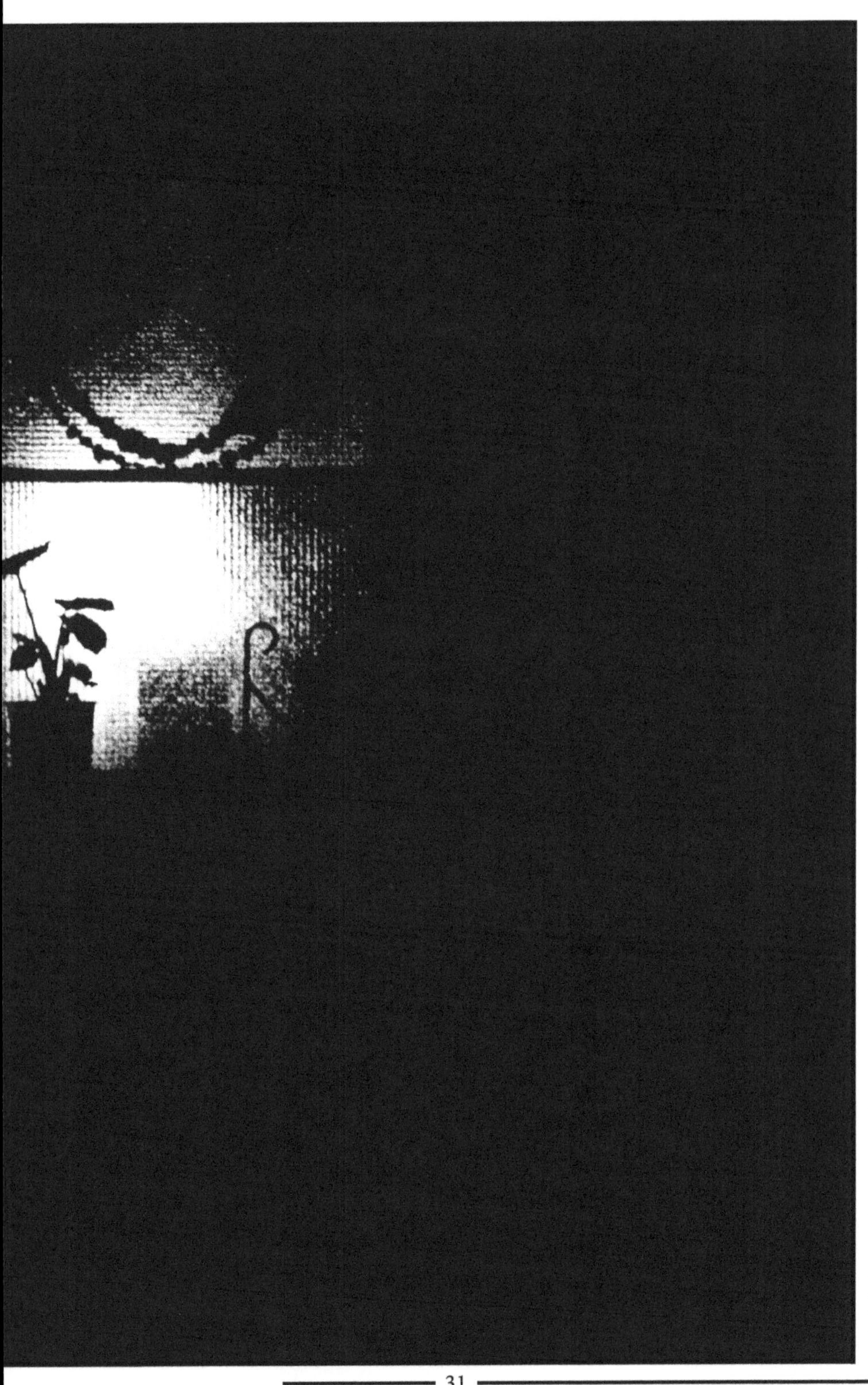

Demeter's Complaint

M. Shayne Bell

She is at the gates again—
The Gates of Hell!

Persephone, Persephone.

She holds the right pillar,
grooved from her touch.
She looks back once—

I would blight
the Earth,
wither it,
crumble its watered gardens
into dust
but for her eyes.

My daughter, my daughter.

Take a basket of apricots. I said:
they are amber like the morning sun—
she asked for a pomegranate.

Take these pears. I said:
they are yellow like the noon sun—
she asked, again, for a pomegranate.

Take one, then. I said:
they are blood-red like the setting sun.

Hermes

Steven Van Pelt

Eyes like two small animals,
Pelvis and thighs mounted
By black spandex, a golden bicycle between
His whirling spindleshanks and knees,

He speeds forward. Direct as a thrust,
This young god is his own herald.
No need for exegesis.
He'll give it as it is

And take what he desires.
Dream on, observer. The wings of sleep
Are for everyman. If cows
Walk backward, then even you

Can grasp your bounty. Yet the god
Will have his sacrifice.

Relevé

Amelia Eilertsen

steeped in reveries of abstraction
lost in a counterfeit painting
the scene is set into action:
a costumed devil sautés in maladroit strokes.

pointed toe facing forward,
arms careened overhead in an arch,
patiently waiting
for the accompanying mark to be hit.

breathing is soft
yet deep with anxious fluttering
coming from the closed curtains
stapled onto a navel-to-neck scarred chest.

behind wire mended ribs dangles a birds cage,
home to a flightless robin
too afraid to flap its clipped wings
during the quiet, contemplative moment.

music swells at the venom spread of a hornet sting,
the concerto burgeons into a magnetite cocoon,
offering a rising tempo, quickening faster
and faster as a prerequisite to an ominous premonition.

wide-eyed, touched by hot air
stagnating under charcoal coloured velvet coattails
and steam pressed sequin gowns shimmering bold,
audiences gut foam filled armrests with polished fingers,
sipping on exquisite vodka and lime

and savouring the sweetness of
crushed maraschino cherries in a wine spritzer.
meanwhile the masquerading devil ensnares,
his touch,
callous.

epileptic caresses stokes further movement.
writhing, struggling, bucking hard fist to
hollow cheek and drawing
scarlet in a fevered rage,

the chase never lets up.
the string tied shackles
unseen in daylight hours
impossible to break free from.

delicate steps
invoke the essence of innocence,
of unfolding fragility like manila coloured cashmere
beneath a forgotten hot iron spotted with burnt nylon.
sacred dances of opposite nature,

choreography escalates into crusade,
movements lost of delicacy,
traded in for a show of distress
and the after-effect is delight.

the masquerading devil's movements
always a step behind
overshadowing every silhouette it touches or towers,
morphing into faceless black masses.

whetted gasps leave mouths agape,
the single violin in the tin and nickel
orchestra screams through the hot air
in a dense, flat note.

the miasma of alcohol and excitement permeates
off the red rows of cured leather seats
condensing into thick sweat that rains from high brows
under noble arches.

faint, beautiful melodies cantering off a grand piano
are drowned out by the cacophony of chaos
-distortion of the devil's symphony.

the staged skirmish grows more desperate,
movements becoming less fluid, more forceful.
as the climax fast approaches,
the gilded robin strains under the lacy corset.

swinging its tired leg from front to back,
tilting its upper body slightly backwards,
it poses,

the black mass hovers over,
lips obstructed by hard, red plastic
but sneering all the same.

with a chaste kiss, both bodies tumble to the ground,
folding like the water starved stem of a
flaccid rice grain.

the music stops,
the violin's string snaps,
curtains draw in for the close.

the main stage lights turn on with a shuttering echo
and suddenly the whole theatre is stripped of its silence

marked by thunderous applause,
the play has ended,
the roles have reversed.

Positioned

Christy Prahl

She of the tawny ponytail, the lacquered peach toenails peeking through sandals, tenderly. She of the hydrangea bushes, of the godsend Carmella who comes twice a month to tidy the house, of the silver hatchback plugged into the electric socket in the garage - don't put your fingers in there, it will burn your hair to barn straw - of the handmade masks she routinely forgets to carry into the supermarket. She of the Mandarin immersion classes for tiny Amelia, who plays the violin, poorly, to great acclaim. Of the shelter spaniel mix nearly left for dead at Animal Control. Of the inherited Waterford goblet collection (not her style but you can't exactly throw them away), the cities burning on CNN while she bakes a blueberry pie. She of the morning meditation to her dead father's Joni Mitchell LPs, of the industrious red wigglers in the composting bins, the single clean finger checking for polyps inside her panties, snuck sideways for the pleasure she suspects she doesn't deserve.

Finding Within

Lee Felty

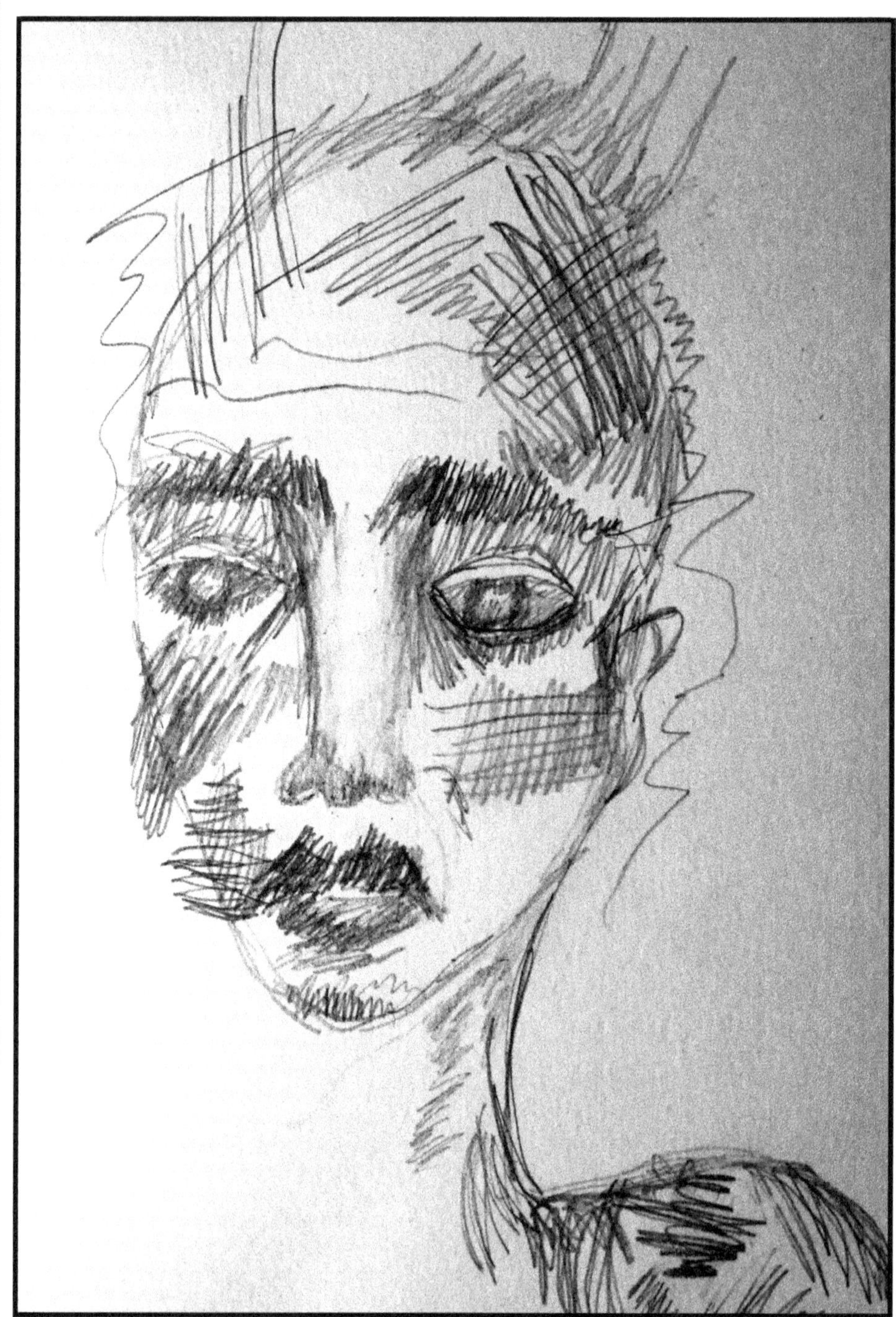

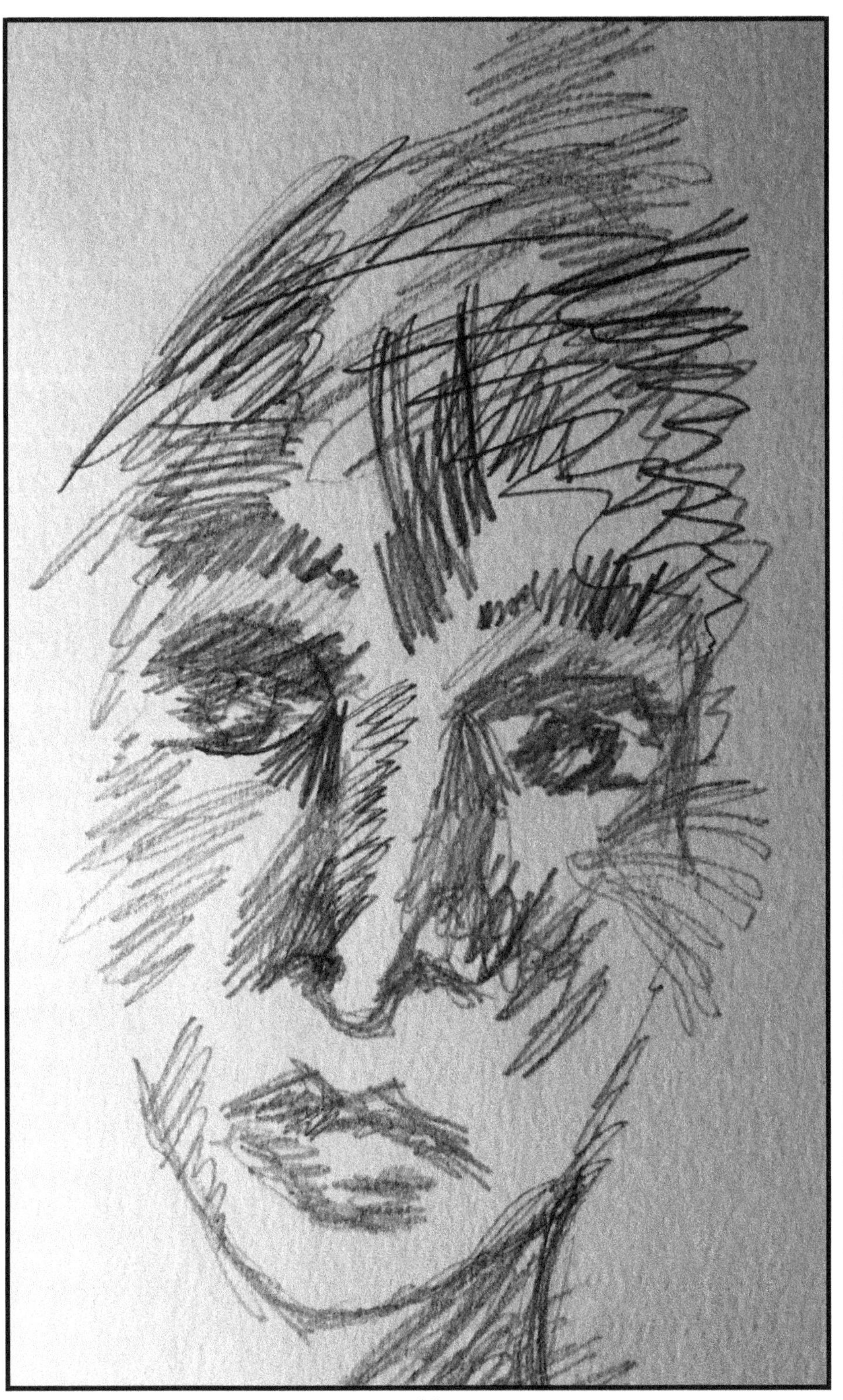

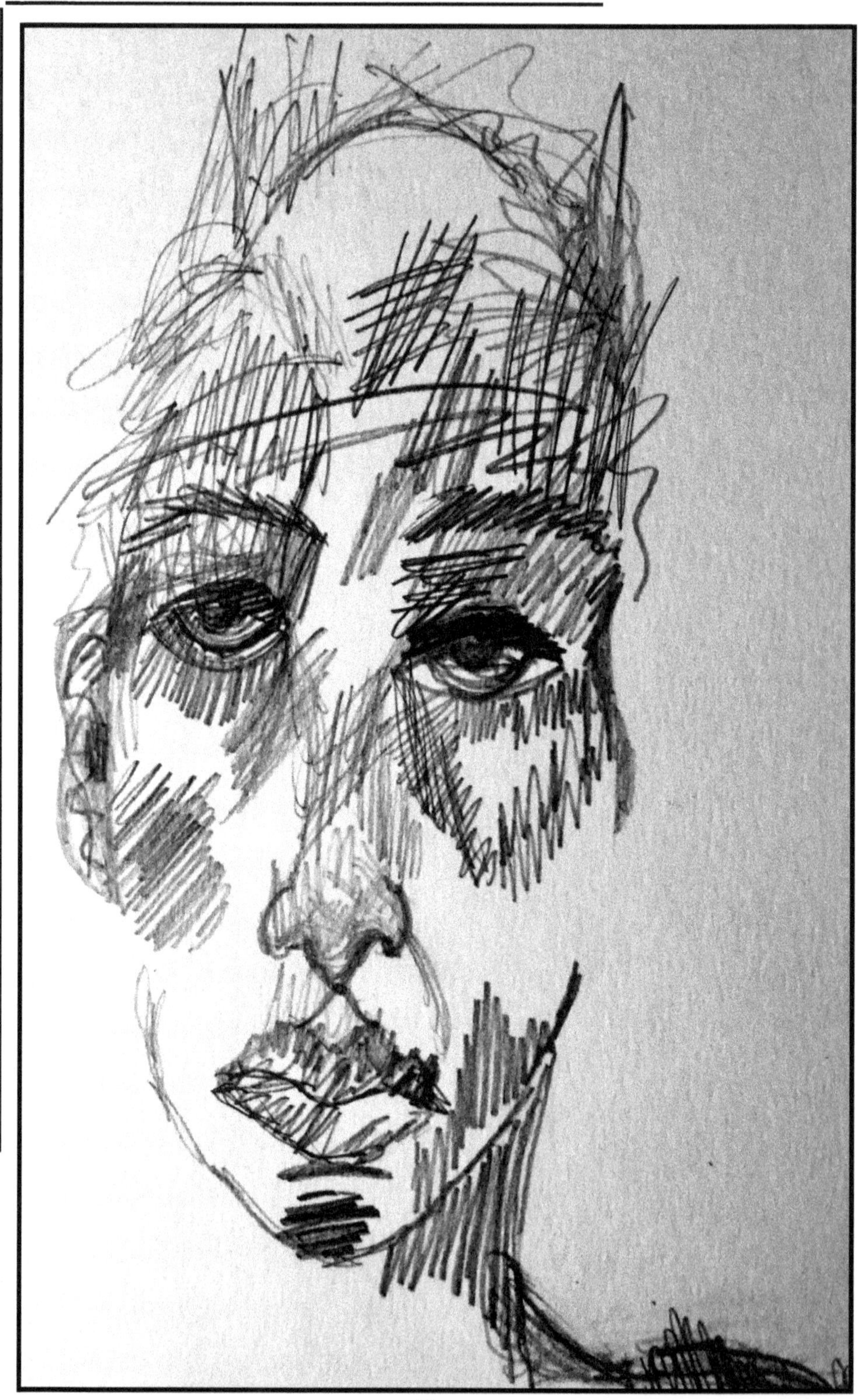

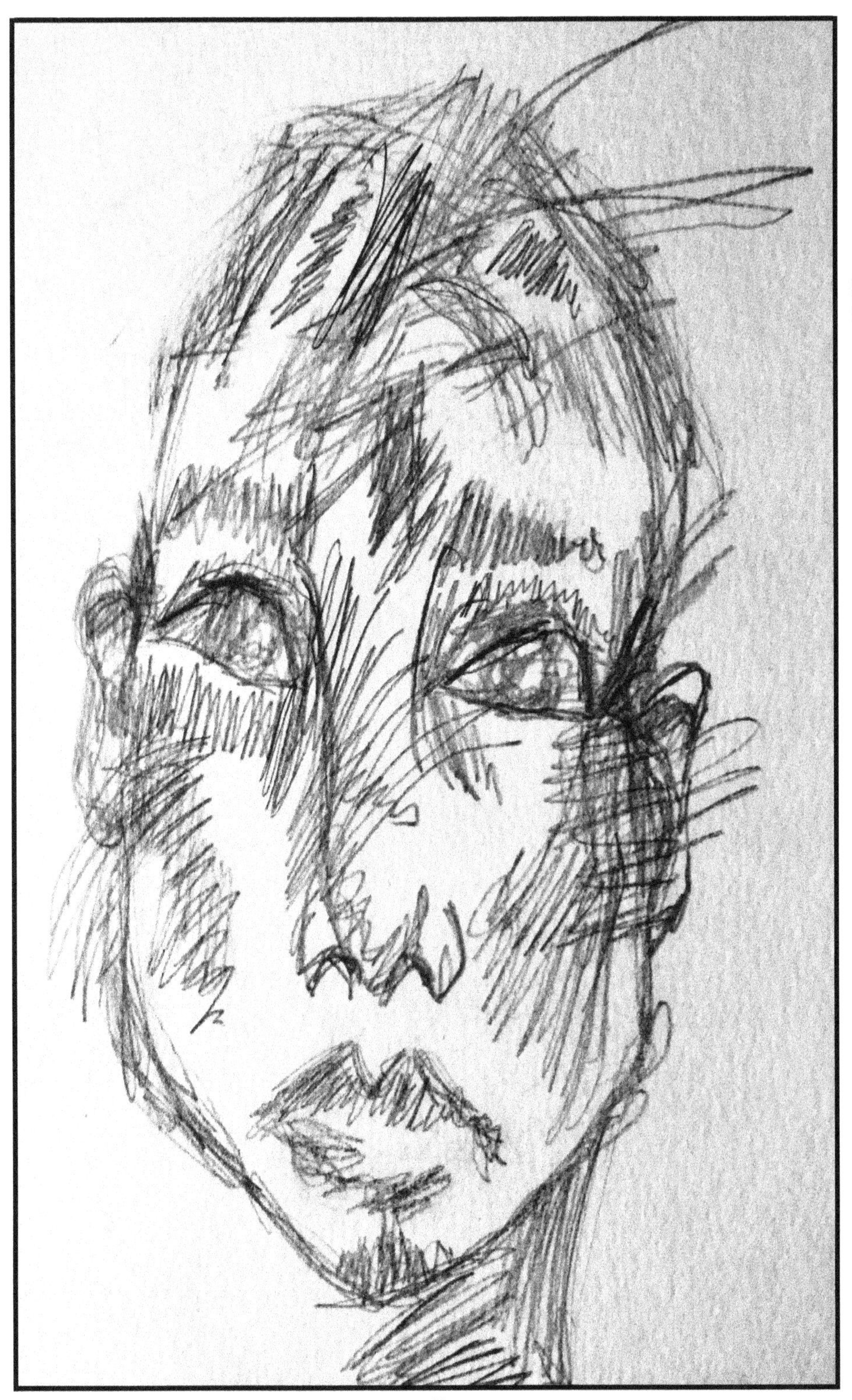

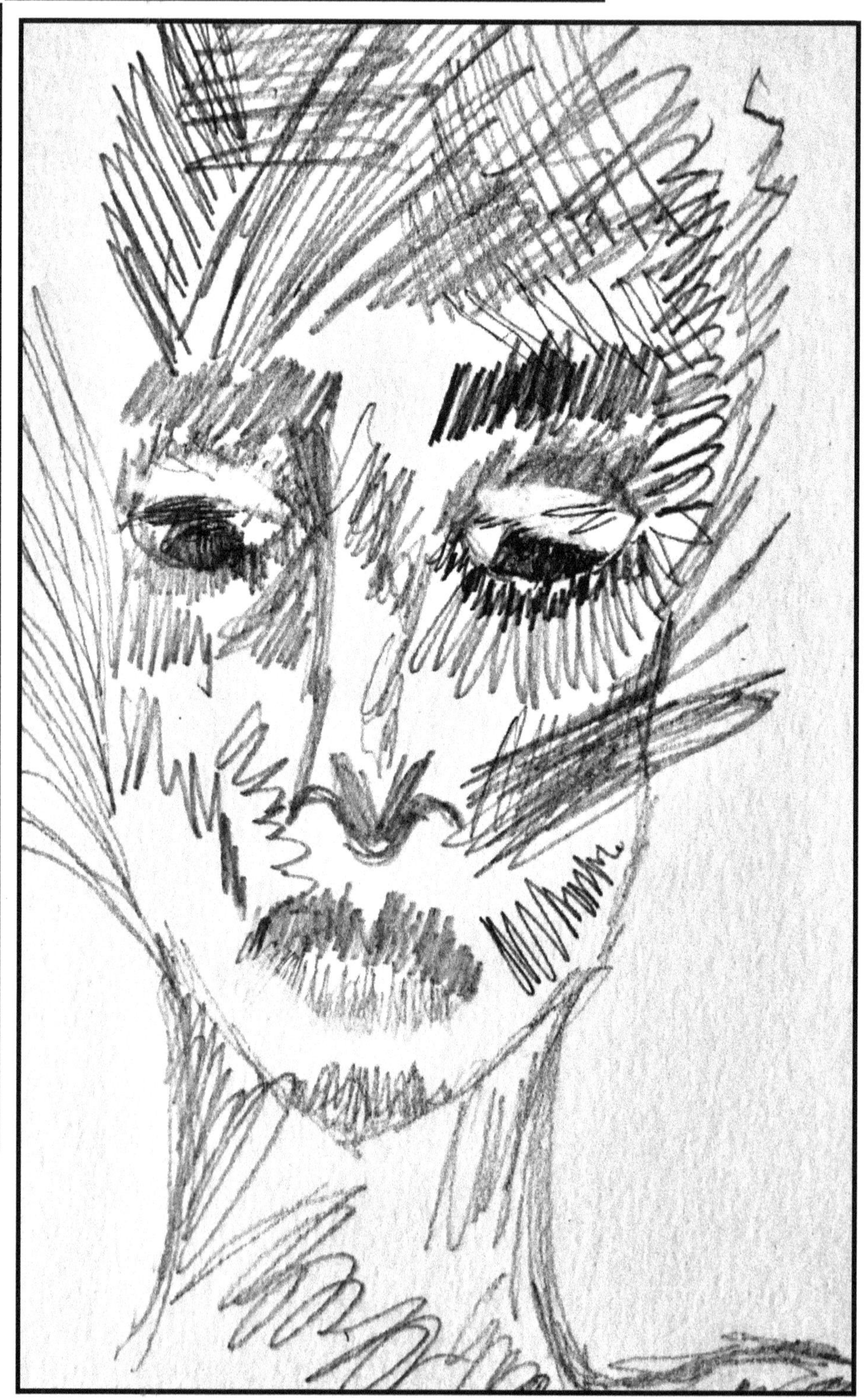

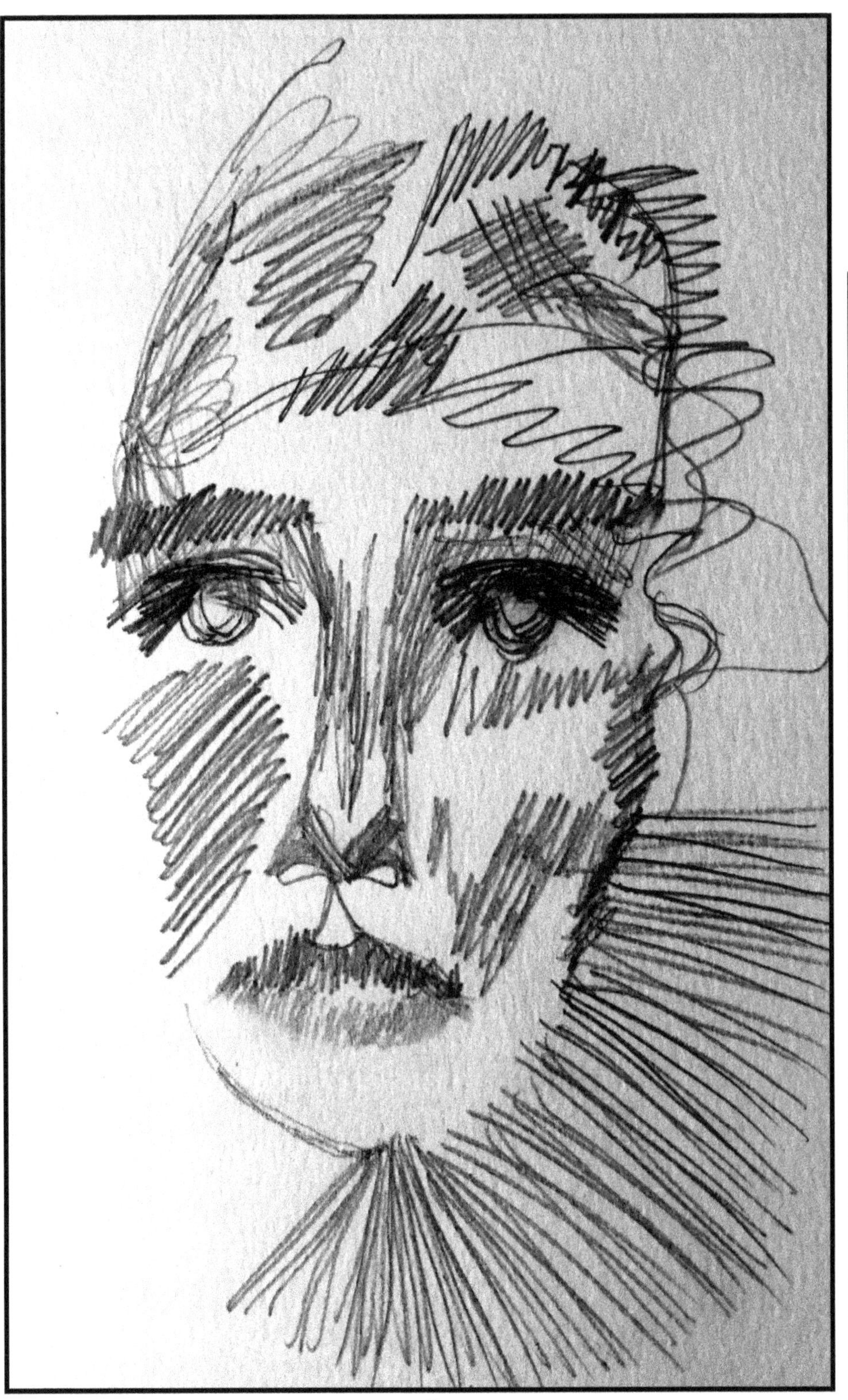

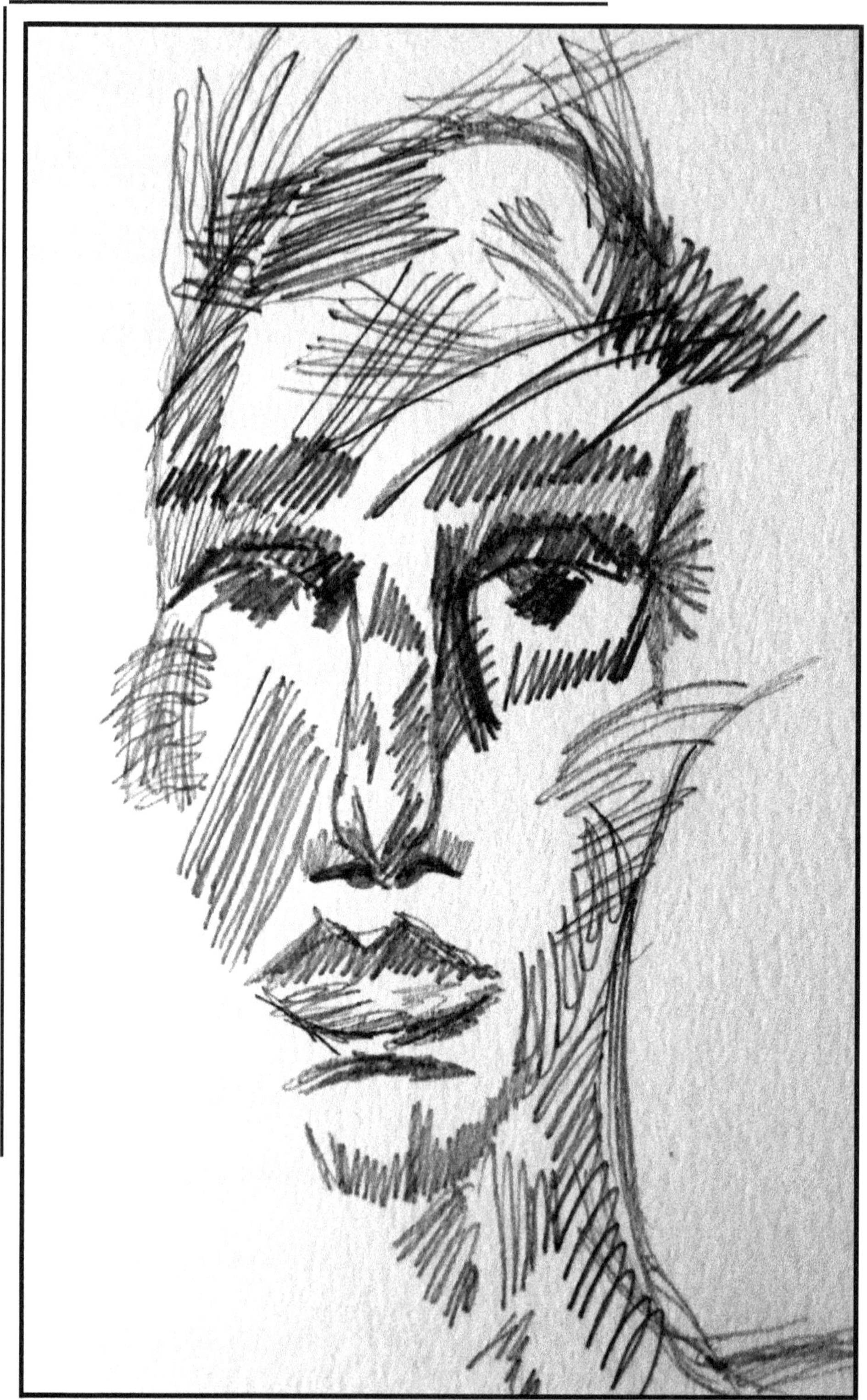

All My Feelings Are Numbered…

Mark Rein

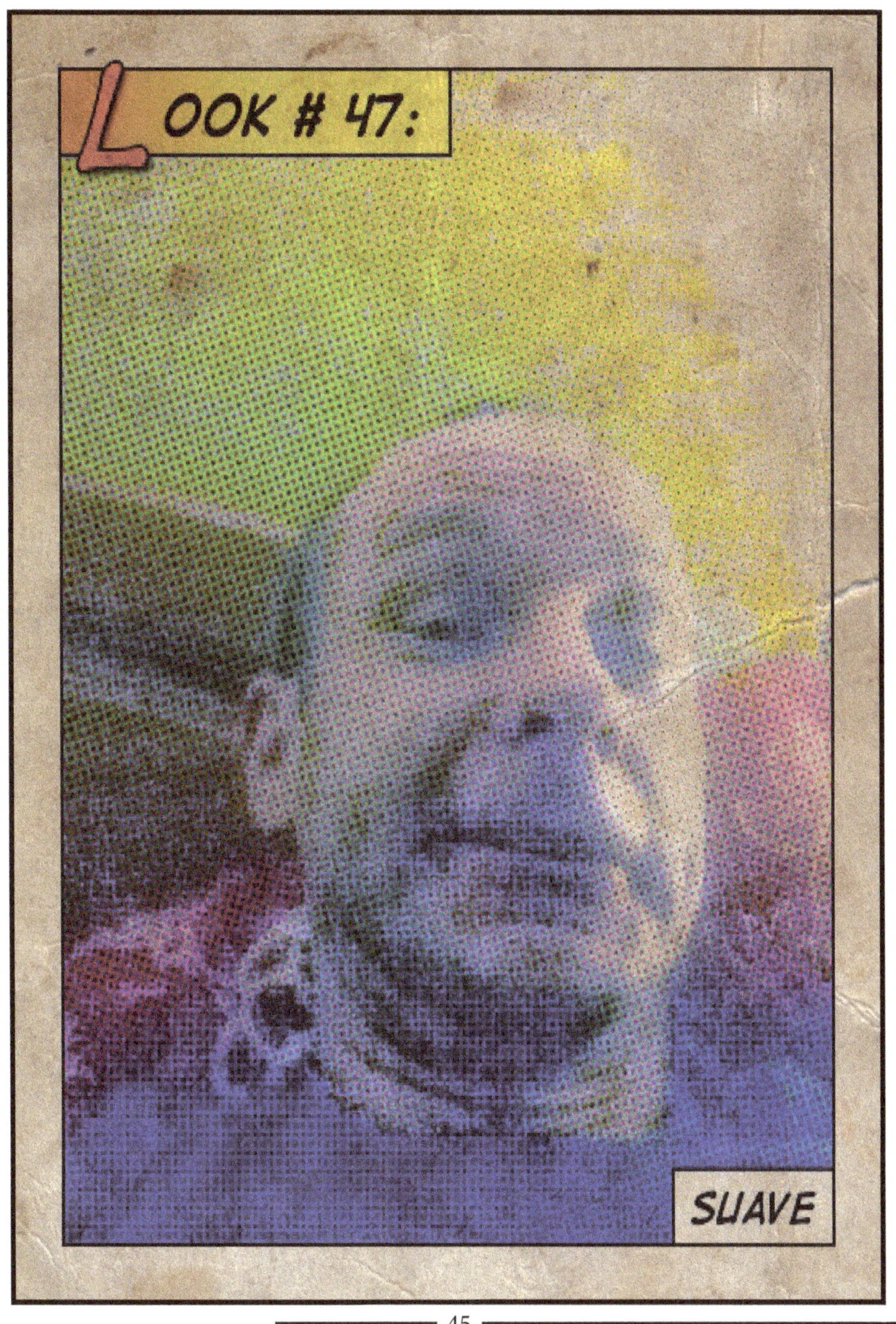

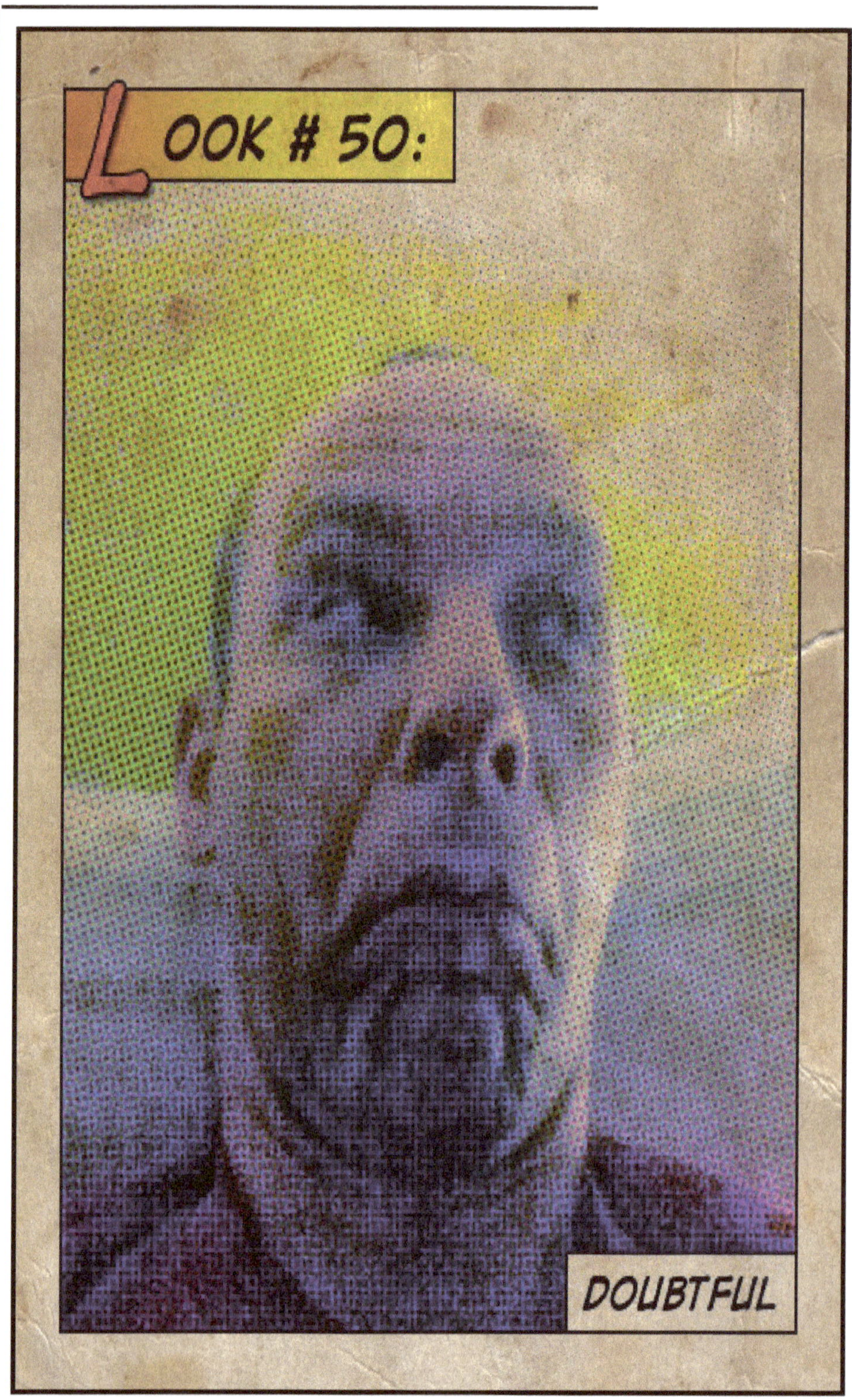
LOOK # 50:
DOUBTFUL

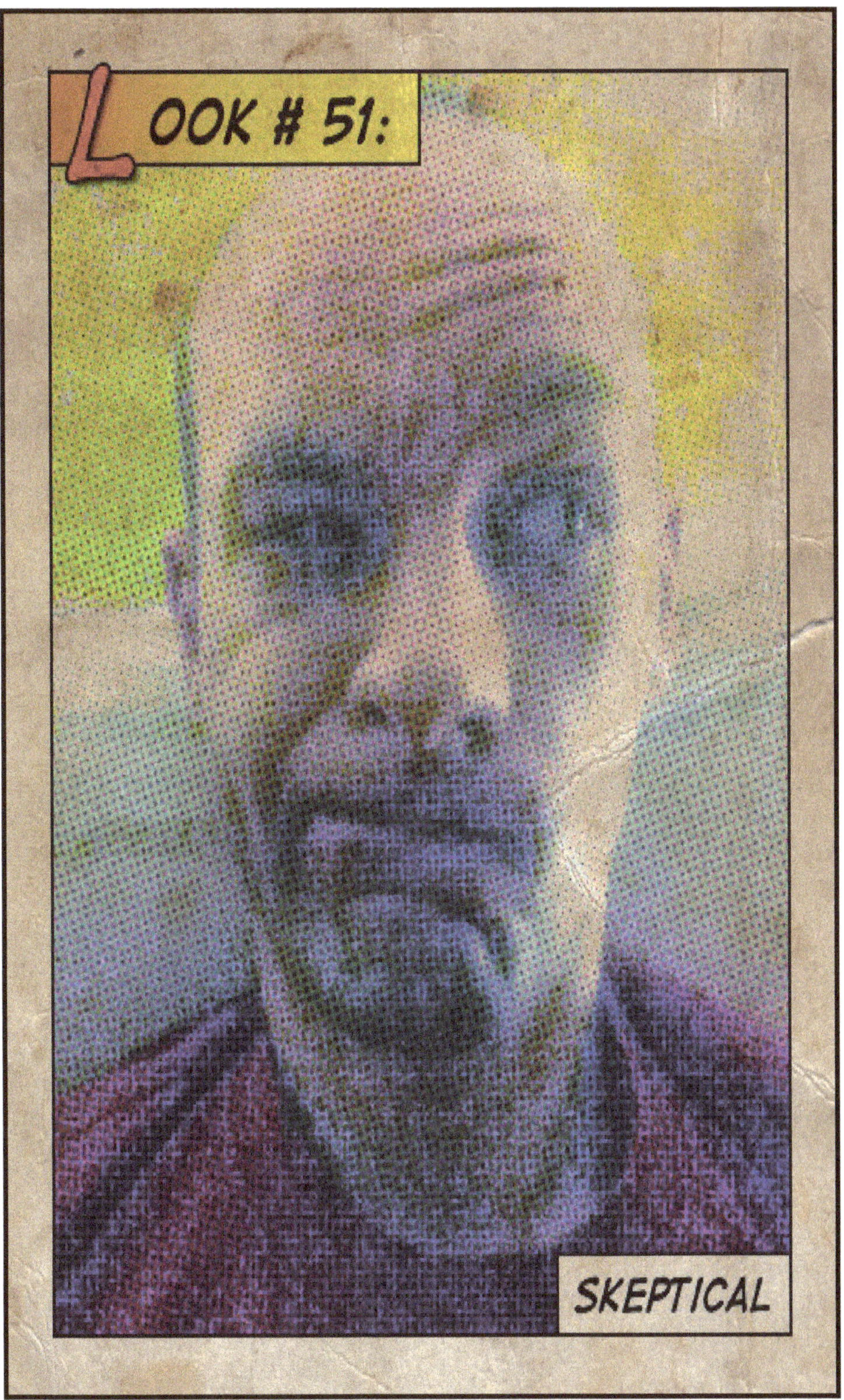
LOOK # 51:
SKEPTICAL

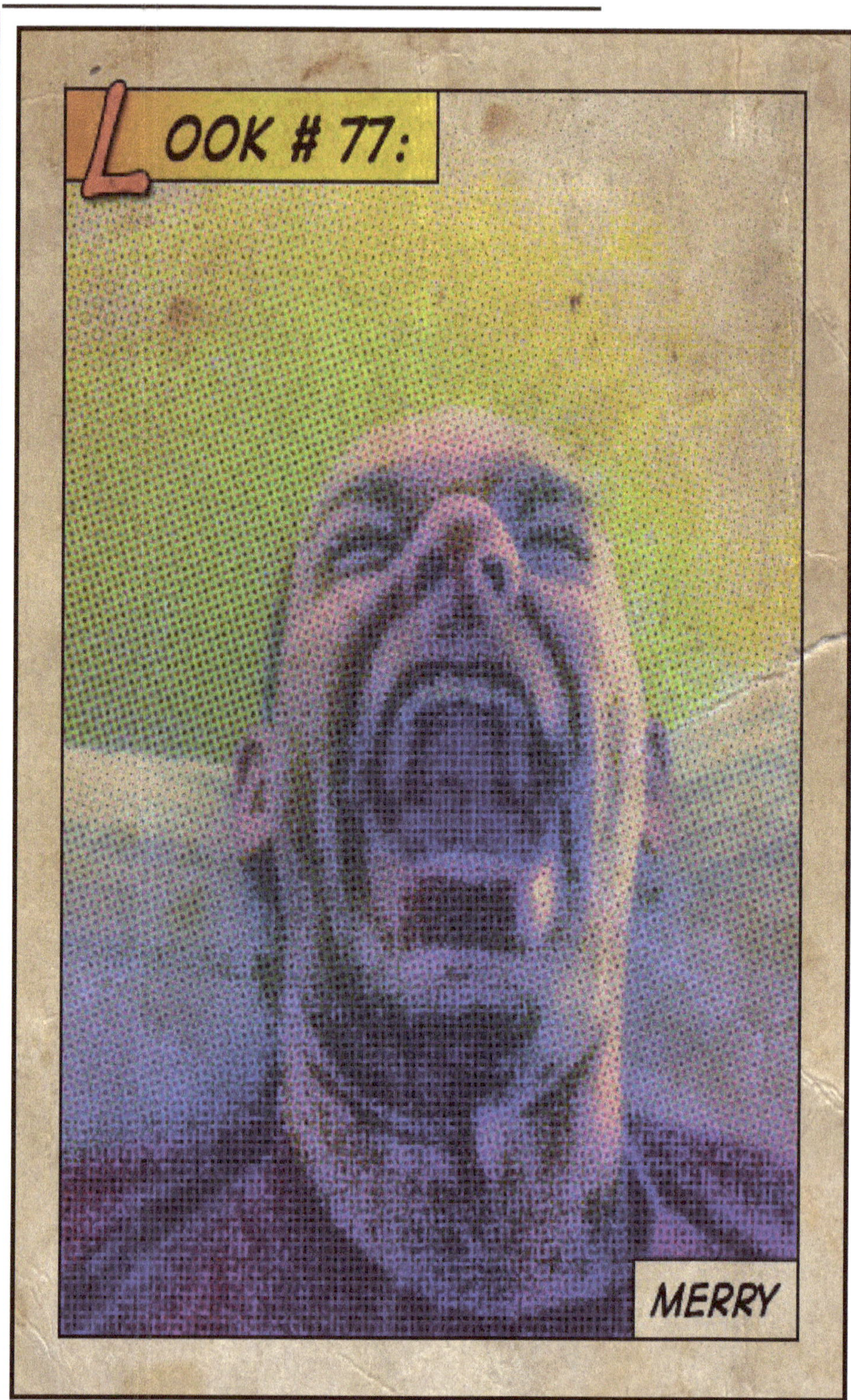
LOOK # 77:
MERRY

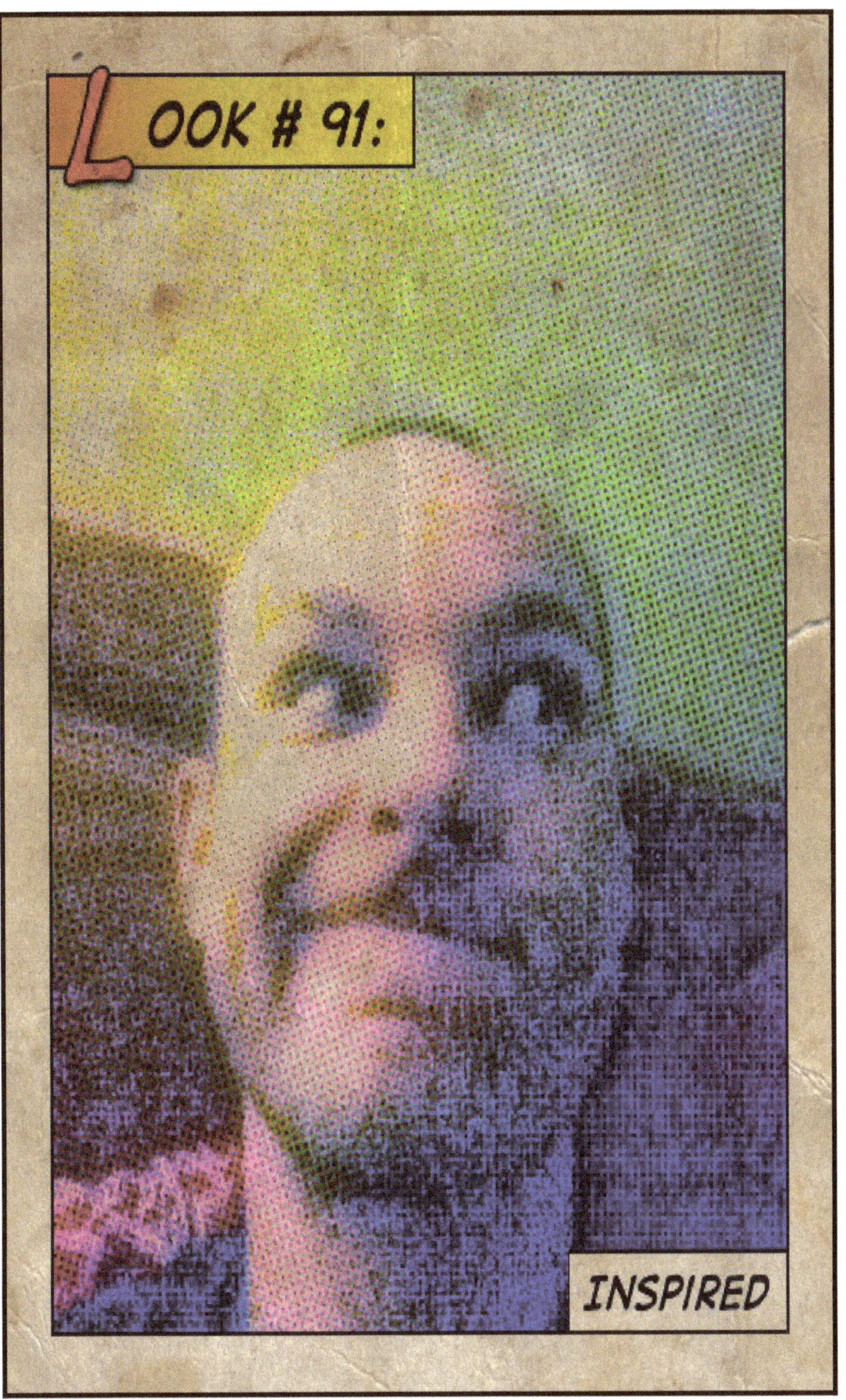
LOOK # 91:
INSPIRED

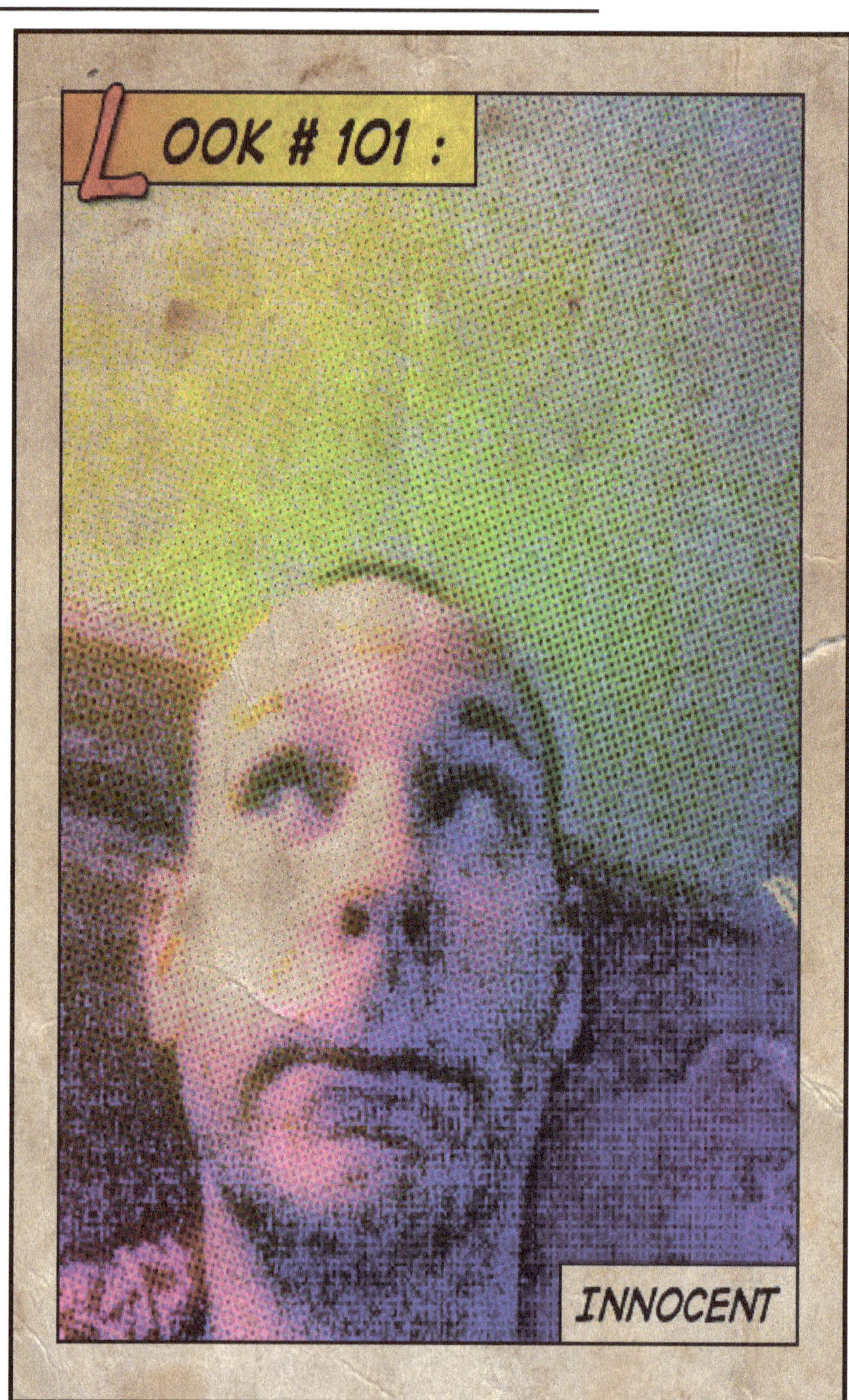
LOOK # 101 :
INNOCENT

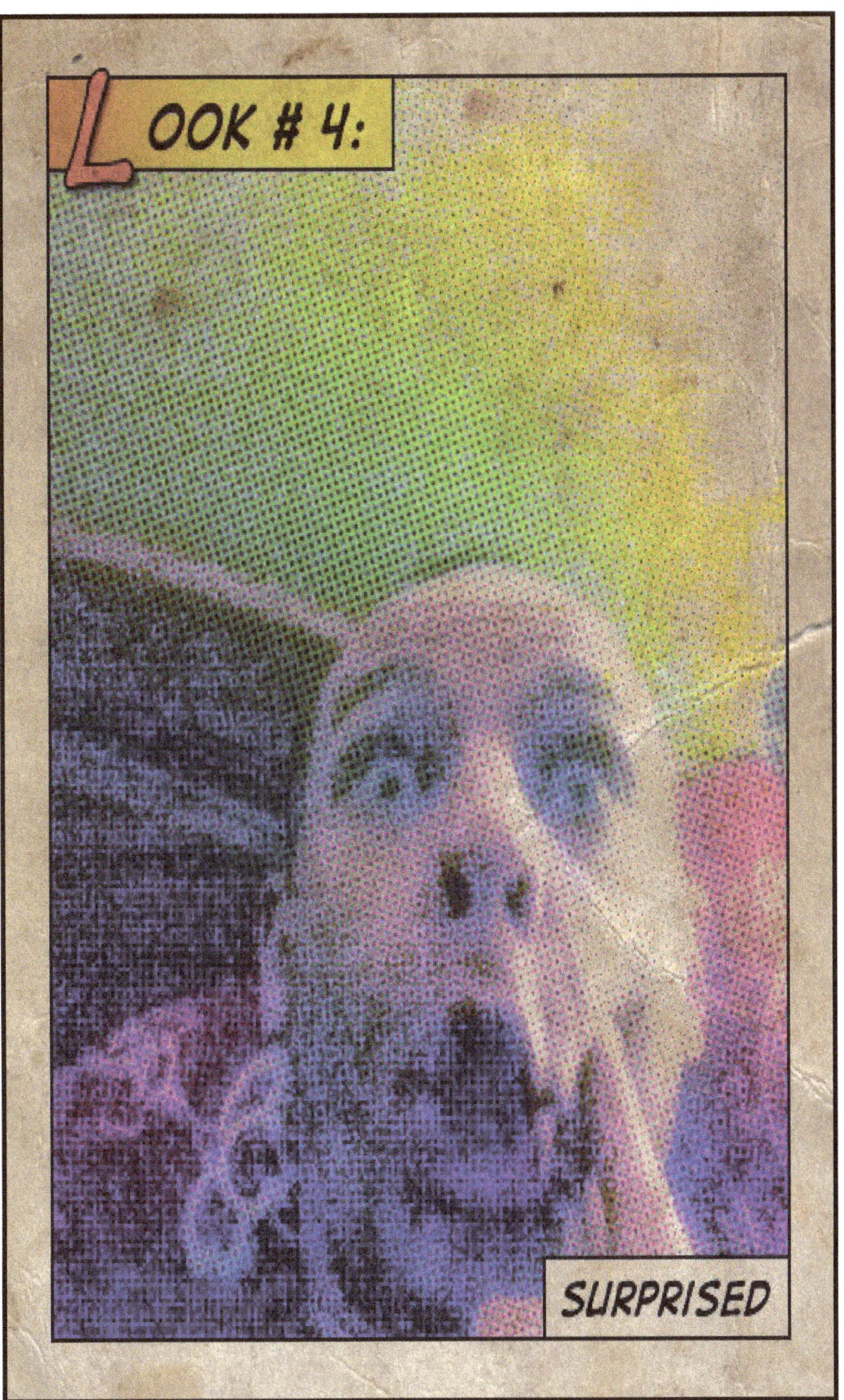
LOOK # 4:
SURPRISED

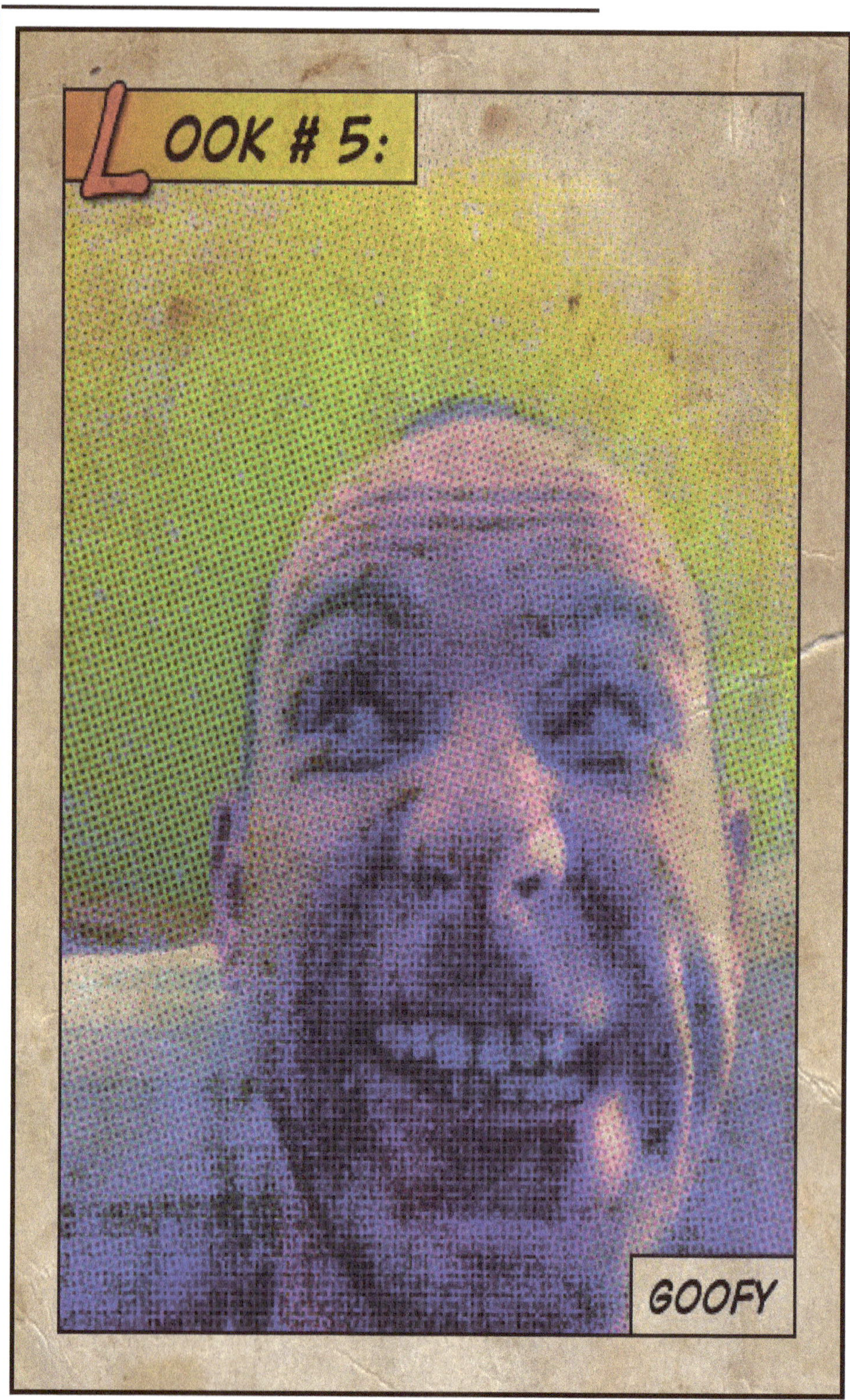
LOOK # 5:
GOOFY

Requiem for the Lactose Intolerant

Neil Izenberg

In answer when asked what foods I missed most
since finding out there can be no more lactose

Some changes in diet have made me bereft.
The foods I once loved are the foods I've now left.

Ring, in their honor, my sad dinner bell.
My requiem calls. So hark. Heed me well.

Baguettes spread so thickly with fresh creamy butter.
For that, I gave thanks to some generous udder.

Cow, sheep, and goat cheese. You granted my wishes.
You tickled my palate. You flavored my dishes.

[Including most products of lactating mammals,
such as buffalos, yaks, and Bactrian camels]

Quiche named Lorraine, our most favorite type.
I Insta'd your photos, sent texts, and did Skype.

Bagels with schmears of Philly cream cheese.
Tomatoes, some lox, always certain to please.

Drafts of full-strength, dark chocolatey milk.
Drunk in great gulps, like cold liquid silk.

Chantilly and schlag and heavy whipped cream.
As soft and as sweet as a wee baby's dream.

Banana cream pie in Graham cracker crust.
Some donuts and cronuts. Cannoli. All bust.

I stand and salute you for what you have done.
We've had such good times. We've had cramps. We've had fun.

So let's dip our forks to that which is gone.
Bow heads for a moment and bid them bon bon.

Thanks for your servings. They must all now surcease.
Dairy departed, let us digest in peace.

WHEN A GRATIN BECOMES A GANACHE

Fred Pierre

I depend on blogs, online influencers and cooking websites for my daily eats. When I need to whip up mousse or steam bibimbap, I turn to the internet. There's a recipe for everything. So of course I was one of the first people to wonder if something had gone terribly wrong.

The first clue was my overly salty Saltimbocca. The recipe came from Cooks Illustrated, so I was sure every ingredient had been carefully tested in their kitchen laboratory. So why was my sauce so salty? I had to throw the whole dish out. I chalked it up to human error and moved on.

It wasn't but a week later that I had another disaster. I was watching @evelyncooksamerica. Her soufflé video made the result look fantastic. Her kitchen was well-lit and spotlessly clean, but something was wrong with the recipe. The soufflé was excessively spicy and I only had minutes before the guests arrived. I dumped a bunch of pasta in a pot, heated some store-bought tomato sauce and managed to serve up a simple plate of rigatoni. The dessert didn't taste quite right though. The recipe hadn't called for a sweetener!

I blamed social media culture. Why would someone post a recipe without checking the text? I turned to Martha Stewart's website, where the real cooking happens.

Who wouldn't smile, imagining Martha Stewart and Snoop Dogg making sandwiches together? It's dependably heart-warming. That's the same way I feel about Martha's chef-tasted recipes. I know they will delight my guests. But not this time. Her recipe for making a garden sandwich included putting a leaf of lamb's ear between the tomatoes and the chickweed. I almost choked when I tried to chew through the furry leaf. Two days later, Martha posted that her site had been hacked.

I tried my favorite cooking blogs, written by people I trusted, who had been posting for years – the best cookies, the most delicious breads, the tastiest gluten-free crackers, and the most savory Thai curry. Bloggers wrote about learning to cook with their grandmothers, how they explored different diets to get through health crises, and how they experimented to achieve their dream dishes. These were my people. I kept thinking, "One day that will be me." I had a file of food photos waiting for the right moment.

But my problems continued. Baby Food Bistro offered up the world's best baby food, but my baby threw it up. Sweet as Sassafras mixed me a foul-flavored mojito. Literally. It tasted like chicken. Italian Cooking with Angelina had me boil the orecchiette into a gelatinous lump, and Hal's Home-cooked Hamburgers' meat-free cheeseburger crumbled into pieces, leaving my lunch date with a plain old cheese sandwich.

I couldn't catch a break. People were complaining about it online. They posted their monstrous creations, labeled "Epic Fail Flan" or "Terrible Tournedos." It wasn't long before Mark Zuckerberg was called before Congress.

Senator Amy Klobuchar demanded to know why millions of Americans were forced to throw out their carefully prepared meals. Zuckerberg's response was both inspired and insipid. "We've identified some bad actors on the platform. We're currently fine-tuning our algorithms to eliminate problematic recipes."

Dozens of cooking sites revealed that they had been hacked. For many, it meant developing new recipes or finding physical documentation of Grandma Ione's Avgolemono Soup. Chefs had to revert back to the three-by-five recipe cards of their ancestors, many of which were too food-stained to be readable.

Home gourmets like me didn't have a lot of options. Even the sites we trusted were being actively manipulated. No one knew how long the Great Cooking Calamity would last.

The president called for calm and instituted a national ban on cooking from scratch, but by then even most of the industrial recipes had been diluted. It was hard to detect the changes because the best recipe hacks only altered one ingredient.

I felt utterly bereft without recipes I could rely on, but then I remembered my grandfather's mantra that had gotten him through the yam famine, "Turn that crisis into an opportunity!" So I turned my gaze within. I could be the trusted source for recipes! I got out my three by five cards and started writing.

Every day I could feel the social fabric coming apart at the seams.

The divorce rate increased as husbands and wives became embittered over asafoetida and tarragon, and many children subsisted solely on mac and cheese. Famous chefs went bankrupt and celebrity cooks were outed as abusers when they couldn't pay their beleaguered staff. The whole food industry had to rebuild from the ground up.

We never found out who launched the attacks. The hacks were traced to a remote location in the Ukraine, but a live-streamed SWAT raid on an abandoned Wonderbread plant revealed only two dust-covered web servers with the hard drives wiped.

The whole experience brought about a rebirth of cooking. Young people spent hours on the phone with grandparents, asking about family traditions. Braggart chefs ate humble pie and returned to the airwaves more bashful and compassionate. Many people closed their social media accounts and joined secure sites like "Crypto Cooking" and "Safe Bytes." Food was in the news every day!

And I finally started my own cooking blog, where I present blockchain-protected, taste-tested favorites like General Tso's Tofu, gluten-free madeleines, and Salade Niçoise with mock tuna. I explain the difference between a gratin and a ganache and encourage sharing and discussion, because food is about community. It's about connection. But, damn it, I've got to keep on top of the comments, because one "too salty" can torpedo the entire thing.

Wellness

Mark Elgersma

After talking on the phone with a gloomy Halpatty protein engineer for the last 70 minutes, Samantha finally was able to hang up. Her stomach grumbled. Through every choked sob of her most-recent horribly depressed caller, she couldn't help but crave one of the free-range-flavor "meat" substitutes that he had worked so hard to create. Samantha stood and stretched, looking around the crowded room.

She was only one of two-hundred Synchronous Help Desk Assistance Specialist and Team Members—SHDASTMs—in the stark-white cubicled chamber. Samantha had been brought on to route calls for her employer, RemoteSource, when the employees of client companies called. Initially, she acted as operator for RemoteSource tech support, maintenance, and dozens of other services.

However, in response to many client companies losing profit from their employees committing suicide, RemoteSource had started to expand their horizons very soon after Samantha had been brought on. After a quick contractual change, the client companies' employees could also call with personal grievances, searching for emotional support. The SHDASTMs' duties expanded to accommodate these calls. Samantha, after a thirty five minute training video, was certified as an official "RemoteSource Emotional Support Professional and Expert" and was given a tin badge to identify her as such.

While Samantha listened to the crowd around her, a growing electric whir identified the approach of Mr. Man. She turned to distantly greet him, hoping he would finally leave her be.

Mr. Man was an unsightly mole on the already-pockmarked skin that was Samantha's worklife. He, an automated manager and shift supervisor, was a chrome cylindrical roving drone equipped with emotional intelligence simulation software and an encyclopedic knowledge of management strategies. When Mr. Man spoke, it came out as a singing tenor that enunciated every letter of every word.

"Why hello, Samantha VanderHarren-Ino, how are you this fine afternoon?" He asked.

"You can just call me Sam. Or Samantha. That'd be fine."

"Yes! I understand where you are coming from. Your emotions are valid and something to be celebrated! However, as there are many Samanthas and Sams that we employ, I regret to say that, to promote clarity and communication in the workplace, I believe it would be best if I were to refer to you by your full name! So no! But remember: your emotions and frustrations with this and all situations are so valid, and the RemoteSource family wants to encourage your individuality!" A small screen on Mr. Man's front lit up with a pixelated smile and "YAY" underneath.

"Alright," Samantha said flatly, "I'm going for food."

"Wait, Samantha VanderHarren-Ino, I would like to discuss something in my office with you! Would you like to have lunch? I shall get the company to provide some. Food serves as a wonderful bonding experience between coworkers! We can build a good work relationship, promote team connections, and increase job satisfaction."

Samantha thought for a moment. She tried to avoid Mr. Man whenever possible, but she also severely needed to save money, and a free meal was hard to pass up. After a moment, she spoke. "Fine. Let's go."

Mr. Man flashed a thumbs-up on his screen. "Fantastic! I'll lead the way." Then he turned and began to roll down the aisle.

One of Mr. Man's many flaws was his inability to go any speed but slightly slower than an average walk. As such, anytime he asked someone to follow him, it led to them trudging.

By the time they reached his office and Mr. Man was behind his empty desk, Samantha's forehead was slick with sweat. Behind Mr. Man, a floor-to-ceiling window showed the large snow-ridden city of Bilnaujaat. Bilnaujaat--previously known as Naujaat before it's sponsorship and expansion by Bilco--was one of hundreds of sponsored compact settlements that were established in the arctic following America's drought, now referred to as the "Big Shrivel." Samantha, along with 95% of North America's population, now lived above 55°N. Each building in official compact settlements was required to house a certain number of people both above and below ground and be fully reliant on green technologies. Each one of these buildings, above its primary entry way, bragged that "the way of the future is together!" It was also this togetherness that forced Samantha to sleep in the same room as Hellen, a fellow SHDASTM who was birdish and smelled of celery. Samantha looked around Mr. Man's office. Two of her apartments could have fit in here.

"Did your weekend consist of a comfortable level of excitement, Samantha VanderHarren-Ino?" He asked after a moment.

It didn't. "Sure," she said.

"Excellent! Now that rapport has been built, I would like to discuss a raise with you."

As Mr. Man said this, a panel slid silently open on the wall, and a steaming Halpatty with Verisco Chips was presented on a plastic RemoteSource-branded tray. As Mr. Man had no orifice with which to eat, Samantha safely assumed that this was hers. She took it and sat in one of the two minimalist stools in front of the desk. It was then that she realized what Mr. Man just said. "A-a raise?"

"A raise!"

"What kind of raise?"

"The kind in which," Mr. Man said enthusiastically, "you don't get one. In fact, your pay shall be lowered. We've recently noticed a drop in your mentions of RemoteSource-sponsored products, and as such, your per-hour rate will reflect that!" He flashed another smile.

"What?" Samantha asked, "I've mentioned every required product umpteen times over. I keep a list next to my desk."

"Yes, and grand job of mentioning every one of the old sponsored products. But now, Samantha VanderHarren-Ino, we're on to a new, sleeker list of sponsors, now nearly double the size of the old one!"

"When was this?" Samantha said, her eyes glazing over again.

"Nineteen days ago," Mr. Man said.

"And how was I supposed to know?"

"It was very clearly stated," Mr. Man said, "in the RemoteSource hourly company newsletter number 22956. We sent it directly to you."

Samantha opened her mouth in anger, then closed it. She could feel her face grow hot.

Her emotions had been tempered by a feeling of dread. The window behind Mr. Man was barraged with sleet and snow at all hours. Even now, on a relatively mild day, wind whipped between the gray, utilitarian buildings plastered with advertisements, raising a fog of ice that hung over the entire city. The streets, no matter how well-lit by LEDs or well-shoveled by solar-powered plow-drones, were a void. The options for Samantha VanderHarren-Ino were a reverse-raise or death. If she could get to the south, she could maybe live long enough to find another job, but right now, she hardly had enough money to get down the road. She bit her lip. "Okay," she said.

"Wonderful!" Mr. Man said, "now finish your delicious Halpatty sandwich quickly. As we provided lunch, we've shortened your break by five minutes. Enjoy! And good luck on the lines, Samantha VanderHarren-Ino. Remember: We care about you, and you're bound by contract to do the same for us. The future is bright!" Another smile, and then Mr. Man turned and rolled out without another word.

"The future is bright," Samantha muttered to herself, "the future is bright."

She ate her cold sandwich as she stared out the white window.

El Paso

Amanda Hartzell

Do not suffocate. Do not send your children
across the border on tricycles intended

for outer space. A name can make
you less a person, more a crater.

Bunker down in the orbiter eyes north
with everything designed to burn beneath.

Greetings from interplanetary dust, from
its spectral frost on asylum and prickly pears.

Where else to go but towards inevitable
uncertain dark — even the youngest sense

meteors in El Salvador, then a hopeful wreck.
The world ends in spectacular blues

and citrus, in a picture from childhood
cutting into sprinkles on birthday cake.

The one blanket given: woven from stardust
and traded by gangs for milk. What's English

for America? Do you need your blanket?
If you're hungry and cold

list right now the birthdays of anyone
who has ever touched you.

Intimacy is a shock to what the body trusts —
Don't comprehend body. Understand space

spreads into a deeper gaze. No dates and
no end. Just unwashed elbows. Suddenly

deepest sea makes sense, the windowless
room and its bodies in silver wait,

all pressure and anonymity.
Brachiopods in desert. Boulders cut

from hickory by glaciers. Limestone
as conduit, a uterus in the warehouse.

There is nothing left but everything. A howl
forgotten in a cage. Counting by twos.

If the world ends without cake or children stand
up tall, burn the pictures, learn foreign words.

Libretto

Adriana Rewald

Relish what mouthwork
my non-mother tongue
requires, deposited once more
on this half-mother soil.

Recede into cobbled
semi-knowns, made-my-owns,
arias ripped from local tones:

remarks stackable as back roads,
the hidden-pocket phrase stash,
decades honed, so I can pass
as here-grown, my personal
apocrypha polished
by this mouthbound
pumice stone.

Spit out pigment, unfurl
the vestigial bones;
avoid appearing counterfeit,
unclasped, or in any way overtly
un-homed.

Progressive

Leon Fedolfi

Differentiation draws a following -
then cures itself. White blood cells
follow the brands you put on cattle.
You have to be alive a few decades to realize -
real change is the one you fought for,
and later built a fence around.

How are you feeling? In that backyard Montana.
That fall through the sky, the trajectory of your life.
Not good, a man named Jim, replies.
On his horse,
fenced in
by his belt and buckle.
His feet never finish on the ground.

He is looking for a young bride -
a new mirror.
He has a sales pitch,
and will sell the land he thinks he travels.
Thinks he owns.
He wants the land you walk on.
Something changed, but not really.

Bourbon Cheeseburgers Gasoline

James Redfern

she studied the receipt.
took a drag of bourbon.

bourbon
cheeseburgers
gasoline

she set up the hose.
opened the kitchen door.

three dogs charged into the garage.

"go for a ride?"

she poured the cheeseburgers out in the backseat.
the dogs piled in.

she slid in beneath the wheel.
shut the driver's door.

she turned the motor over.
let it idle.

the dogs tore into the paper-wrapped burgers,
and the driver worked the bourbon with abandon,
but long before the bag and bottle
were empty and gone,
they all drifted off to sleep.

she left no note.
only the receipt.

ROSEMARY / REMEMBRANCE

Art by Ann-Marie Brown

Words by Milo Merrill

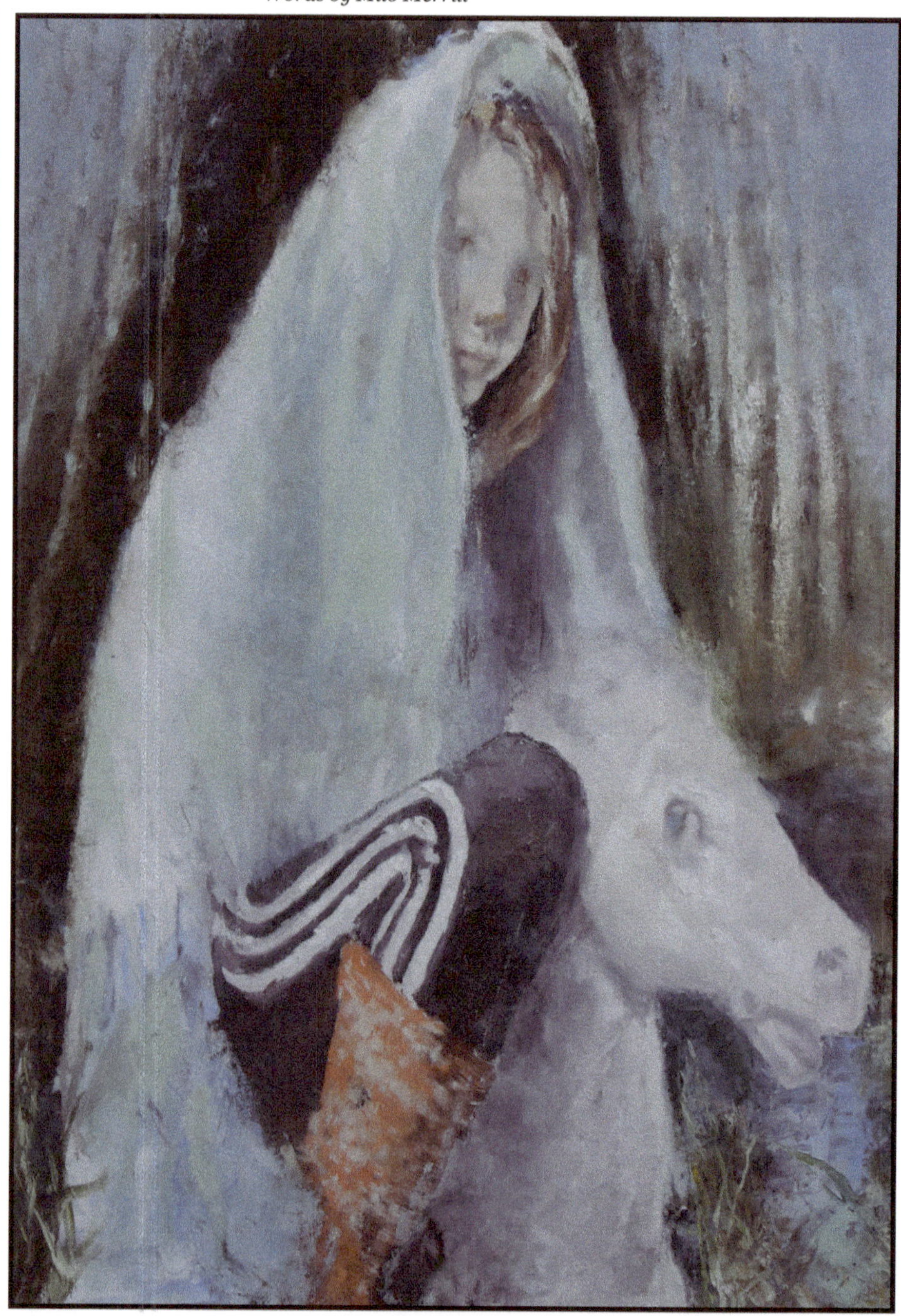

do you remember Omelas, or did we forget when we walked
away from the — tattered skin and bone oh,
darling have you found yourself yet have you found the
HOME you meant to before the guilt and — tore it all to shreds,
that is — do you remember going HOME or already being
HOME and making broccoli cheese soup from a can for lunch
and did it give you absolution when you saw your reflection
in the silver spoon or did you have to find the river first?
do you remember Shalott, little lady? are you running wild,
little lady? usually i only think about Death alongside his brothers
and his whores, but now i think i got that part wrong.
do you remember Ophelia, how she would never have swallowed
saltwater, how she bloated and bubbled blue in the water?
i bet you found her beautiful and closed those glassy eyes for her,
two fingertips on her eyelids all full up. did you grow the fennel
just to kill it, little lady?

In Order Of Appearance:

Katie O'Malley is a current undergraduate student at Southern Methodist University studying English and Education. She loves reading and writing and hopes to pass on these passions to any future students she may have.

Seneca Basoalto boasts two B.A. degrees and a background in the backstage music/movie scene – where she's adapted her graphic experiences to fuel the evolution of her craft. Seneca's audacious temperament and bisexuality can be seen influencing the attitude and magnetism of her diverse range of work.
Her writing has been published in England, Scotland, Australia, and the United States with appearances in collections through NAILED Magazine, Terror House Magazine, Utterance Journal, North of Oxford, Breadcrumbs Magazine, and Glasgow Review of Books.

Dualtagh McDonnell was born in Dublin where he currently resides. He studies English and Drama Studies at Trinity College Dublin. and enjoys writing and reading things that provoke thought. @dualtagh_

Kimberly Patino is an American photographer and visual artist. She received her BA in 2013 from Hunter College, where she studied literary criticism and fine art photography. Patino began her career at portrait photography company Glamour Shots where she honed her skills in portraiture and artistic imagery. Her work focuses on topics that revolve around women, identity, body image, and the relationship between Americanism and her Hispanic roots. She's exhibited in solo and group shows to include: The Greenpoint Gallery, The 440 Gallery, The Bowery House, The Harrison Public Library, and the One River School of Art and Design. Patino has been published in various mediums including ARTSNEWS, Feature Shoot, Canon, and Adobe's Twitter. She currently lives outside of New York City. Follow her recent works through Instagram @kimberlypatinoo

Signe E. Land earned an MFA in Writing from the University of Minnesota and a JD from William Mitchell College of Law, graduating class valedictorian. She taught creative writing at St. Olaf College and the University of Minnesota and practiced law in Minneapolis. Ms. Land's work has appeared in William Mitchell Law Review, Bookends Review, Rivet: The Journal of Writing that Risks, Atticus Review, Lady/Liberty/Lit and others. In 2019, Ms. Land won third place in the Kay Snow Poetry Competition, Second Place in Atticus Review's Flash Non-Fiction Contest, and was nominated for a Pushcart Prize in poetry.

Ann Pedone graduated from Bard College in 1992 with a degree in English Literature. She has a Master's degree in Chinese Language and Literature from UC Berkeley. Ann's work has recently appeared in, Neologism, Ornery Quarterly, Unbroken Journal, Alba, Riggwelter, Main Street Rag, Poet head, among others. She lives in the San Francisco Bay Area.

Though born and raised in a small farming community in rural Nova Scotia, Kristen Herrington has called Halifax home for more than a decade. She is a prolific abstract painter and designer, with a particular interest in collaborative works. She studied -what she calls- the artist's "thing" for her Master's thesis as an avenue to explore the relationship between the creative individual working in a capitalist society. Through this research, Kristen discovered her own "thing" and has been working on that artistic evolution for the past 6 years.
She identifies as a fluid-artist, capturing life's overlooked moments or ideas on her canvasses. Additionally, she explores the raw and vulnerable nature of the female form. She has worked as a nude model for her local arts university and has recently collaborated with her photography friend and co-collaborator, Lyndsay Doyle to bring a gritty take on her "other" personality.

After a decade in the corporate world, Lyndsay made the leap to full-time entrepreneurship in 2012 so she could make her own rules. With a headstrong and quirky personality, Lyndsay approaches her work in a straightforward way, taking care to relay strong social messages with her art through humour and honesty. Her photography and writing clearly show her passion for social justice issues, particularly in the field of women's rights. Whether through subject-based projects, or through self-portraiture, she weaves art, business, and audience interaction seamlessly, while focussing on projects that specifically aim to break down barriers for women, celebrate their strengths, and create discussion.

Samuel Keith Bliss is a photographer and writer living in the leafy north of Melbourne, Australia. His work is often centered around his home, drawing narrative from the sublime Australian landscape as well as the gritty reality which hides beneath the surface in his working-class home.
Samuel has previously been published in 'Rabelais' magazine of La Trobe University, where he is currently completing his BA in English and Visual Cultures.

M. SHAYNE BELL received a Creative Writing Fellowship from the National Endowment for the Arts (1991).
Bell's haiku have been published in Modern Haiku, Frogpond: Journal of the Haiku Society of America, The Heron's Nest, The Wales Haiku Journal, Blithe Spirit: Journal of the British Haiku Society, Tinywords, Sunstone, Shot Glass Journal, star 82 review, O:JA&L, Haikuniverse, and Mainichi Japan (where his haiku were listed among the best English-language haiku of both 2015 and 2017).
Bell's poetry has also been published in The Ghazal Page, Cathexis Northwest Press, The Fibonacci Review, Kind Writers, High Shelf, Shot Glass Journal, Typishly, Dialogue, Asimov's, and Once Upon a Midnight (an anthology commemorating the 150th anniversary of the publication of Edgar Allan Poe's "The Raven").
Bell's book of poetry based on Greek mythology, "Blood Red Like the Setting Sun: Poetry of Hellas and Underworld," will be published by Assure Press, Fall 2020.
In 1993, Bell backpacked through Haleakala Volcano on Maui, from the summit to the sea, retracing an expedition Jack London went on in 1911. In 1996, Bell was part of an eight-day expedition to the summit of Kilimanjaro. Bell grew up on a ranch outside of Rexburg, Idaho; he and his six cats live in Rexburg.

Steven Van Pelt began writing poetry as an early adolescent. After receiving a BA in English from the University of Wisconsin, Madison, Steven was accepted into the poetry division of the writing program at San Francisco State. Rather than attend, Steven moved to NYC, studying dance with Erick Hawkins and, then, for many years, at the Merce Cunningham Studio. Steven continued to write poetry, teaching in the NYC public school system for 20 years, specializing in literacy. Currently Steven resides in Chicago, studying and 'playing' tai chi, reading and writing poetry. Steven has been published in Sisyphus (Hip Pocket Press).

A bleeding heart with a tendency to tilt at windmills, Amelia is a creative writing graduate with an honours bachelor degree in Creative and Professional Writing from Bangor University. Sparked into activism by current world events, Amelia scrutinizes the world around her and critiques the infrastructures of politics, social hierarchies, patriarchal influences on women's livelihood and matters of inequality through her poetry. Ushering from a sleepy town in Norway, and having spent most of her youth raised in Zambia, travel and temporality are her two constants. As such, she grew to appreciate the power of putting restless thoughts to paper and enjoys other hobbies such as photography, painting and running a blog.

Christy Prahl is a writer of a certain age, foraging enthusiast, and occasional insomniac. Her poetry has appeared in the Blue Mountain Review, Cathexis Northwest Press, Twyckenham Notes, and is forthcoming in eMerge. She is also the editor of the literary collection, "A Construction of Cranes" (Plastic Flame Press, 2020. She lives in Chicago with her husband and their plain brown dog.

Lee Felty is a published artist living in New England, USA. Her works focus on the human face. She began drawing seven years ago. In her youth, she was influenced by the works of Picasso, Miró, and Chagall. Complex structures in art are a fascination for her. In her artwork, you will find movement in stillness, moods within stoicism, and often, sadness and grief. She works on her art during the day and at night, sleeping when she finds a need. There is never music playing. There is no magic time of day. When she works, she is focused, lost to the work. If she can be frenetic with her hands as in the works in this issue, she finds her success for there she finds her art's energy.

Mark Rein has been very creative from an early age. He has always written things down as they come to him, from nonsense poetry to short stories.
He dabbles in art; painting and drawing frequently at his home in Sydney.

See his work here: https://www.instagram.com/art.reinman76/
He enjoys painting, but more than anything loves goofing around when he has a camera nearby. In-between family life and having a regular job he absorbs himself in these creative pursuits regularly.

Neil Izenberg MD – until recently a pediatrician, filmmaker, and founding editor-in-chief of KidsHealth.org – is a writer based in Philadelphia.
Izenberg has written and edited a score of books for families about children's health, a multivolume encyclopedia about diseases and conditions for teens, various academic studies, and hundreds of online resources for parents, teens, kids, and educators. Neil served as an advisor and a program developer for a range of organizations reaching families, including Sesame Workshop, Cheerios, the AMA, the CDC, Procter & Gamble, Sprout, the NBA/WNBA, Seventeen Magazine, and the Michael Phelps Foundation, among others.
Izenberg has received numerous juried awards for his work, including 3 Emmy nominations, 4 Webby Awards, the American Academy of Pediatrics Education Award, and dozens of top juried awards for film, print, design and innovation.
Now, Neil is knee-deep writing a collection of short stories of how bites of food and gulps of drink, consumed at just the right time. can change the trajectory of life in unexpected ways and shed light on who we really are.

Fred Pierre writes poems and short stories that celebrate our humanity and our relationship with the natural world. Fred weaves themes from mythology, biomimicry, buddhism and technology into poetic stories that uplift and inspire. This story employs satire to grapple with the pandemic through the lens of a massive hack attack on our recipe infrastructure.
Fred studied poetry and linguistic philosophy at Pomona College and regularly lectures on library technology for the Northeast Ohio Libraries consortium.

Mark Elgersma is a graduate assistant and student at Central Michigan University studying English while focusing in creative writing. He also works as an intern at the Isabella County Human Rights Committee, and his publications include Plain China, Toe Good Poetry, 101words, and more.

Amanda Hartzell received her MFA from Emerson College in Boston. Her work has appeared in New Letters, Paper Darts, Midway Journal, and The Knicknackery among others. Her stories won the Alexander Patterson Cappon Prize and finished as finalists in Glimmer Train.
Originally from eastern PA, she now lives in Seattle with her son, husband, and their dog.

Adriana Rewald is a writer, teacher, and translator who was born in Detroit and raised in Warsaw, Poland. She received her MFA from Hollins University and her poetry has appeared in Artemis, Toho, and on poets.org. She has lived and worked in Virginia, South, Korea, Serbia, and is currently based in China. @adriana_rewald

Leon is an avid reader and aspiring writer of poetry. He was awarded the 2020 Doug Draime Prize for Poetry sponsored by The Raw Art Review, and has published in Rumble Fish Quarterly, High Shelf Press and others. He has a book of poetry, The UnInvented Ear, coming out with UnCollected Press this fall.

James Redfern was born and raised in Long Beach, California. Redfern is a graduate of Grinnell College. His work has been published by The American Journal of Poetry, Transcend, Verity La: The Clozapine Clinic, Dime Show Review, Swimming with Elephants, Montana Mouthful, Anti-Heroin Chic, Great Lakes Poetry Press, Fear and Loathing in Long Beach, Passengers Journal, DoveTales, Into the Void (forthcoming), and elsewhere.

Ann-Marie Brown is a Canadian artist working on the west coast of B.C. on a property she shares with her husband, son, dog, and the occasional bear. Her oil & encaustic paintings have been exhibited across the United States & Canada, and have found their way into public, private & corporate collections.

Milo Merrill is a dog owner, collector of hobbies, and previously unpublished poet from Northern Oregon.

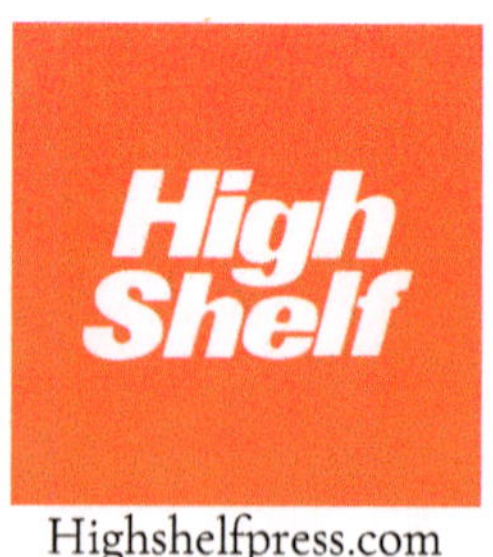

Highshelfpress.com

www.ingramcontent.com/pod-product-compliance
Lightning Source LLC
Chambersburg PA
CBHW050040040726
47599CB00015B/1769